Hello

# Hello
## We were talking about Hudson

*Edited by Steve Lafreniere*

SOBERSCOVE PRESS I CHICAGO IL

Soberscove Press
Chicago, Illinois
soberscove.com

*Hello We Were Talking About Hudson*


The remembrances by Gary Indiana (p. 192) and Richard Prince (p. 187) both appeared in Noelle Bodick, "The Art World Remembers Hudson, Feature Inc.'s Visionary Dealer," *Artspace Magazine*, February 14, 2014.





Names: Lafreniere, Steve, editor.
Title: Hello, we were talking about Hudson / edited by Steve Lafreniere.
Description: Chicago, IL : Soberscove Press, [2024]
Identifiers: LCCN 2023053063 | ISBN 9781940190341 (paperback)
Subjects: LCSH: Hudson, 1950-2014--Anecdotes. | Hudson, 1950-2014--Friends and associates--Interviews. | Art dealers--United States--Anecdotes.
Classification: LCC N8660.H83 H45 2024 | DDC 709.2--dc23/eng/20231204
LC record available at https://lccn.loc.gov/2023053063

ISBN 978-1-940190-34-1
Design: Friendlier
Copyediting/Proofreading: Dan Fox
First Printing 2024
Printed in Lithuania

Distributed by
ARTBOOK | D.A.P.
75 Broad Street, Suite 630
New York, NY 10004
artbook.com

Cover: Hudson, 1993. Photo: James White
Page 1: "Hello," 2014. Drawing: Jerry Phillips

*for*

*Patricia, Jim, Jimi, and Anne*

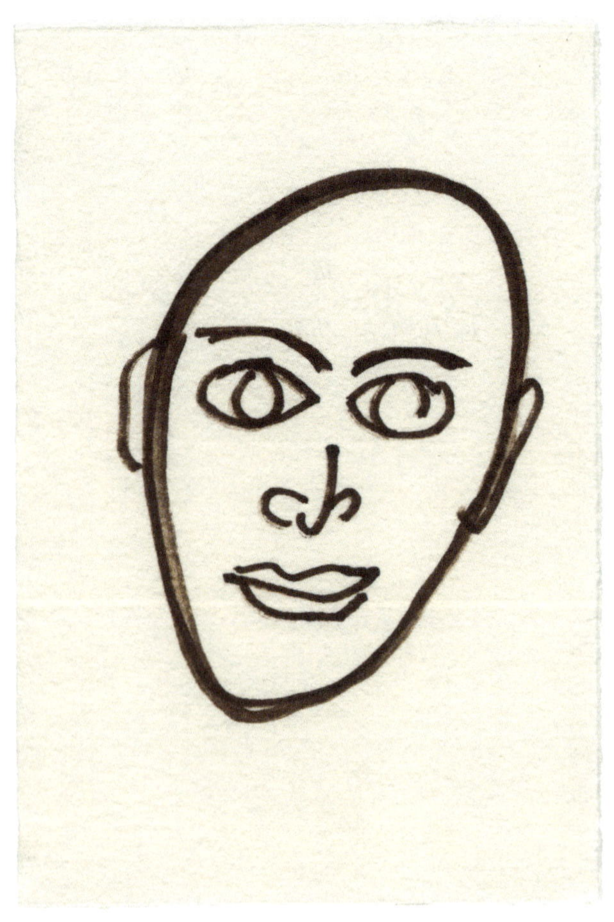

Hudson, drawn by Charles Ray, 2014. © Charles Ray, courtesy Matthew Marks Gallery

# CONTENTS

*Remembrances*



*An interview with Hudson*

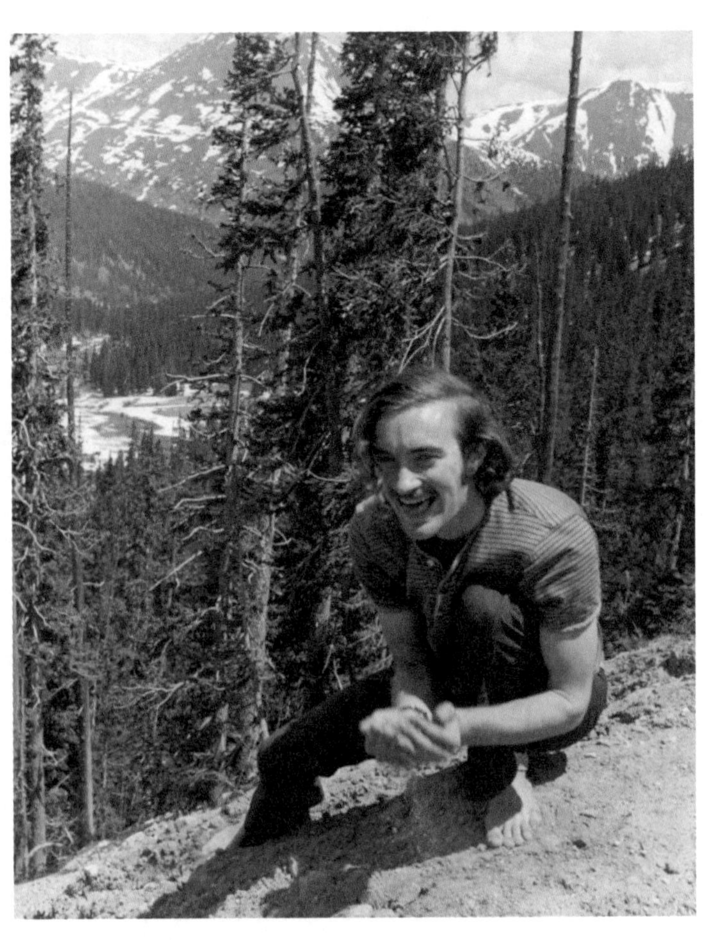

Self-portrait, Colorado, 1969

# PREFACE

*Dear Reader—*

The book you hold contains conversations with and remembrances by those who knew the art dealer Hudson [1950–2014], including artists he exhibited over the thirty-year life of his gallery, Feature Inc. It took shape gradually over a number of years, in the end becoming neither biography nor a comprehensive work of oral history. More subjective and personal than those, it is ultimately a memorial gathering of friends in print.

I worked with Hudson over those decades as Feature's in-house graphic designer. We were also close friends, having met in Chicago before he debuted the gallery there in 1984. Over the last ten years since his death in 2014, the art world in which he maneuvered has transformed. The original spark for this book was primarily my concern to capture and share Hudson's era and efforts for a new generation. I hoped to get down the history of an extraordinary gallery that seemed to run on different tracks than its contemporaries in the larger art world. After some false starts, I realized that a straightforward approach was needed, something Hudson himself would no doubt have prescribed. I recalled the Q&As that he would conduct with artists before their exhibitions, and then offer printed and stacked at the reception desk for visitors to take away. Here was an obvious starting point for a book. I previously had a journalistic sideline doing interviews for arts magazines. How apt to do the same with—Hudson's term—the Feature Creatures. The outcome would be a collection of anecdotes and intimate musings, informal in tone, that would weave together a vital portrait of Hudson and Feature.

While he was chiefly a gallerist, without his own body of static work to examine, Hudson had earlier in life been a dancer and performance art-ist, and as became clear in the interviews, he very much seemed to view Feature as an ongoing artistic endeavor. It was also an endeavor rooted in relations—between him and his artists, collectors, staff, colleagues—and specifically relations that revolved around the physical experience of engaging with art. Throughout the interviews, both of these themes proved to be a subtext to much of what was talked about.

Here are thirty-five interviews, edited for clarity and length and arranged in nominally chronological order—timelines tend to overlap. These are complemented by a smaller second section, an addendum of heartfelt memorials. Some were published shortly after Hudson's death in February 2014, while others are eulogies delivered at the Judson Church celebration held for him later that autumn; a recently written memorial rounds up the segment. And, fittingly, Hudson himself has the last word. Dike Blair's 2007 interview with him has been published before, but as it remains such a candid expression of his sensibility and intent, I've chosen it as a coda.

A few guide notes: In these conversations, subjects occasionally repeat. You'll also find divided opinions and varyingly recalled stories. Rather than smoothing these over, every attempt has been made to retain myriad perspectives. This includes memories that are at odds even with the established timeline. Secondly, though "Feature" and "Feature Inc." are used interchangeably throughout, to be accurate it wasn't until 1994 that the gallery incorporated and changed names. And also, as you'll see, I interviewed myself. Questions that I'd jotted down over years were one afternoon finally answered into a digital recorder. The transcript was then lightly "massaged." Well, Hudson interviewed himself in 1982 [*see page 30*]. Let's call mine an homage to that original temerity, as well as a way of adding my own stories.

I'm indebted to everyone here for their participation. I selected from those whom I'd observed had close histories with Hudson—and in fact, not always smooth going—in different Feature eras, and was gratified that everyone asked was eager to speak about him. Naturally there are many others who also knew Hudson in meaningful ways and whose recollections and insights would have chimed well here. But in the end, this particular mix of conversations and writings covers essential ground and more. At a certain point the book seemed to find a conclusion, and I stopped. However, let this be a nudge to future biographers, scholars, and archivists: There is much opportunity for expansion on this effort, and no doubt a larger story to tell.

Because the book begins with Hudson attending the University of Cincinnati in the mid-'70s, I'm going to finish here with a brief account of his life up until that time.

He was born October 4, 1950 in New Haven, Connecticut, the third of five children. The family lived in West Haven, where he attended public school. In both academics and comportment he was reliably top of his class. Hudson, his sister and three brothers spent their entire childhoods in one house. They were somewhat set apart in their neighborhood by being more observant as Catholics and their parents more strict. Hudson became an altar boy, but after graduating from high school he moved away from Catholicism. His teenage rebellion was a quiet one, reading Anaïs Nin, D.H. Lawrence, and Timothy Leary. He won scholarships to both Wesleyan University and the Rhode Island School of Design. Instead he decided on the Philadelphia College of Art, and finished a Bachelors degree in art education at Southern Connecticut State College.

In his twenties Hudson began a life-long study of Ayurvedic medicine, and a short time later began practicing Transcendental Meditation. He also traveled extensively, living in Switzerland, Arkansas, Nova Scotia, and Washington state. He later moved to Ohio and in 1977 graduated with an MFA in painting from the University of Cincinnati.

---

Hudson died on February 10, 2014, just two months shy of Feature's thirtieth anniversary.

—*Steve Lafreniere*

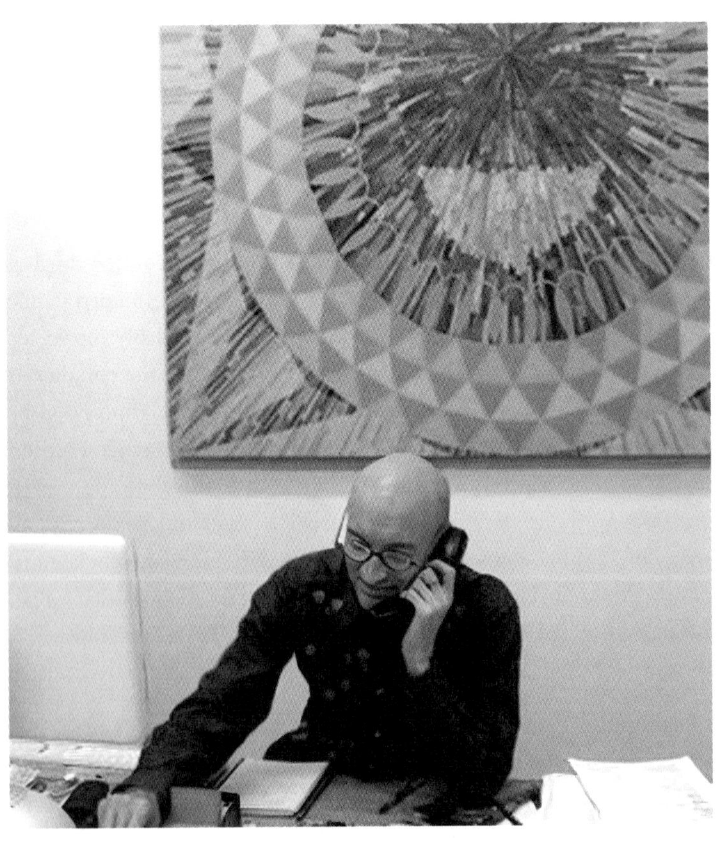

At Feature Inc., West 25th Street, New York City. Painting by Michael Lazarus.
Photo: Steve Lafreniere

## BOB NICKAS

Who in life, looking back on it, far enough along to have a distanced view, was an influence in any meaningful way? As with our closest friends, most of us can count them on one hand. We might only need two fingers. V for victory. We might only need one. The middle finger? A mentor can be also a tormentor. These lessons learned, at times the hard way, are often invaluable, even if you don't realize it at the time, or find yourself resentful in the moment. Real lessons will stay with you as pats on the back won't. Of course a greater recognition will be grasped when it's you who runs the dispensary. Once, midway through a seminar where my students, for the most part, were less than responsive to what was being offered, a more seasoned teacher reassured me: "Something you say in class today may only be of use to them years from now, will be recalled and come back to help them." In an instantaneous world, this world of immediate gratification, there is yet the possibility that knowledge may, in fact, be time-released. Think of a capsule swallowed, its outer shell dissolving slowly, a drug entering the bloodstream steadily, released over six to eight hours. Some ideas, in order to metabolize, may require six to eight years. Patience being the least of it. We aren't even aware of what's happening inside of us. And then, when it hits, had we seen it coming?

I used to joke—and, as with wishes, be careful what you joke about—that when I die it could be days before I actually go, as if saying to the end: "Can't you see I'm busy? I can't be bothered just now." Working, distracted, preoccupied as always, I simply wouldn't have noticed that I'd gone. Hopefully, for the neighbors' sake, even if the new yuppies in my building aren't exactly neighborly, the windows would be open wide.

Had we seen it coming? As with the end of an era, so-called, by the time we've registered its arrival it has already passed. In the years leading up to Hudson's departure, there was the growing sense that the art world we had known for so long had not much farther to go. Even in the big booming '80s, and in what was understood to be the center of the art world, New York, there was still a feeling of community among artists, writers, curators, and gallery proprietors. Some who ran galleries were or had been artists themselves, as Hudson was, and this made them much more responsive to the needs, vulnerabilities, and minds of the artists they represented. From the outside, the New York art world may seem to the rest of the country and the world to be some sort of fortified city-state of culture. This is not necessarily so. And it was even less so in the past. The downtown New York art world, for it has always been below 23rd Street, don't let anyone tell you otherwise, has more in common with a small village. Small town without being small-minded, which is what many had left behind. You pass others in the street, gossip, share the news, stop for a coffee or make plans to meet later. Sometimes you briefly kidnap someone you've met. You go around spontaneously to see some shows. The galleries are nearby. In the galleries the art on the wall is by someone you know. In the galleries you run into other friends and familiars. You share opinions. These "reviews" mean much more than those in the paper, especially the paper of record.

One of the galleries frequently visited was Feature, presided over by Hudson, and presided is precisely the word. One definition rings particularly true: to be the featured instrumental performer. There he was, at his desk, quietly absorbed. He did not rush forward and throw himself over visitors as some gallery owners do. He let people look. Isn't that what we came for? And if we approached, he would engage us in a completely engaging way. He was one of the few who understood what he was showing, what the artist was about, could help you to see. Most other gallery proprietors, in stark contrast, couldn't do that. They could tell you the price, who had already bought the work, to impress or entice. It was only business. You shouldn't have taken it personally.

There was always available a one-sheet, the Feature Q&A. In these Hudson asked questions of the artist to illuminate what they do, while at the same time revealing his own curiosity. I learned a lot from these concise but expansive conversations. It was clear that Hudson possessed what most other gallery owners don't: vision. He introduced us to many artists; many would become friends, a long list to be sure: Lisa Beck, Huma Bhabha, Alex Brown, Jason Fox, Daniel Hesidence, Mamie Holst, Bill Komoski, Lily van der Stokker, B. Wurtz. Late in the gallery's history there was a show titled *Punt, with the Feature Family*. I did think of the gallery as being a family, despite the infrequency, as in life, of seeing some of our relatives, who we still felt close to by way of their art: G.B. Jones, Isabella Kirkland, Kinke Kooi, Judy Linn, Nancy Shaver, not forgetting exhibitions with Candy Darling and Cynthia Plastercaster. (Wend your way through the gallery's exhibition timeline and see just how many women were part of and defined Hudson's world.)

I went to see every show at Feature between the fall of 1988, when Hudson moved the gallery from Chicago to New York, and early 2014. In twenty-seven years, I did not miss a single show. This can't be said of any other gallery in New York, including those with which I have been associated one way or another, having brought artists to them, organized shows for them. I had been in his Chicago gallery on a single occasion, when I had a show with Rhona Hoffman in 1987. In Hudson's gallery I remember seeing works by Jeanne Dunning, Hirsch Perlman, Kay Rosen, and Kevin Wolff, as well as something by Charles Ray in the office. I didn't know any of these artists back then. Had I met Hudson at the time? I would remember that. Was someone there I didn't speak to, out of shyness or habit, following the unwritten code of conduct in a gallery? Had I sensed an invisible but palpable "Do Not Disturb" sign?

With his relocation to New York, Hudson showed Charles Ray in '89,

Raymond Pettibon in '90, Tom Friedman in '93, Rachel Harrison and Richard Hawkins in '96, Takashi Murakami in that same year—the first presentation of his work in the States; Josh Smith in 2003. These are artists who went on to bigger, deep-pocketed galleries, to museum recognition. Looking over the various offerings in the upcoming auctions, I saw a minor Murakami with an estimate of $150,000 to $200,000, a small Pettibon drawing, only 22-1/2 by 30 inches, at $300,000 to $400,000, a large drawing of his at $1.5 to 2 million, a group of eleven Tom of Finland drawings from the motorcycle series, vintage, dating from 1959/60, expected to bring between $180,000 and $250,000. These are the sort of prices Hudson never saw. Had he been the first to show Tom of Finland in New York? The earliest encounter that I recall was a Feature exhibition at the end of '88, *Heavy Action Drawings*. Something remarkable about the gallery was how Hudson could put before us hardcore, though humorous, Tom of Finland images on the very same walls as we'd later find anonymous Tantra drawings—meditation devices arousing very different but in no way mutually exclusive energies. This aptly articulates Feature headspace. How many galleries actually have headspace? The question is neither hypothetical nor rhetorical. It is, as so much that Hudson achieved, meant to encourage reflection. Something he dissolved for me was the space between figurative and abstract art, which today appear, as with politics, polarized all over again. He taught me that it simply doesn't matter what form an artwork may take; it's what happens when you're in front of it that counts, and where that takes you. Not all art, no matter the hype or inflated price, will be transporting. I would happily go back in time to a show of Hudson's in Chicago in '87 that, though known but never seen, confirmed that impulses some would find reactionary should be encouraged, because they can open up to positivity. There had been a major museum exhibition in 1986 at the LA County Museum, *The Spiritual in Art: Abstract Painting 1890-1985*. (This was the occasion when an American audience was introduced to the work of Hilma af Klint, the visionary Swedish artist who is now a bonafide superstar—not that she would be interested in the least.) Hudson promptly mounted a response: *The Non-Spiritual in Art: Abstract Painting, 1985-????.* Such a punk-ass move; a reminder as well that the truest non-believers are also some of the most spiritual and spirited among us.

How did he influence me? Let's go back to the memorial held after his passing, for which I was asked to be one of the speakers, and had to decline. I didn't know what to say. It was still too soon. One of the most moving speakers, his words directly addressed not to us but to Hudson himself, was Hilton Als, who expressed, as I recall, anger and grace in equal measure. I couldn't have managed that. A week or so later I knew exactly what I should have said. It was so simple, yet eluded me in the grief and disbelief that certain passages present, a wall we can't see beyond, impassable. There they were, as resonant in mind as they had been years before, the titles of Hudson's shows that had registered so strongly, tickled me, excited mischief within: *Godhead*; *Head Sex*; *I Am Not Monogamous/I Heart Poetry*; *Trouble Over So Much Skin*; *I Want That Inside Me*; *Skulture*; *The Sun Rises in the Evening*; *I Gaze a Gazely Stare* (from Bowie's "The Man Who Sold the World"); *Another, Once Again, Many Times More*; *Hairy Forearm's Self-Referral* (his "sequel" to *Hairy Forearm*); *Itsy Bitsy Spider*. From the ridiculous to the sublime. Were they at times not so dissimilar, flowing freely together? I might not have memorialized Hudson, acknowledging my debt to him, his welcome tinkering with my brain, at that gathering, but I do now and with the understanding that an end is not what it seems to be. Hudson continues to influence me and always will. And I'm not the only one.

*—Bob Nickas, writer and curator*

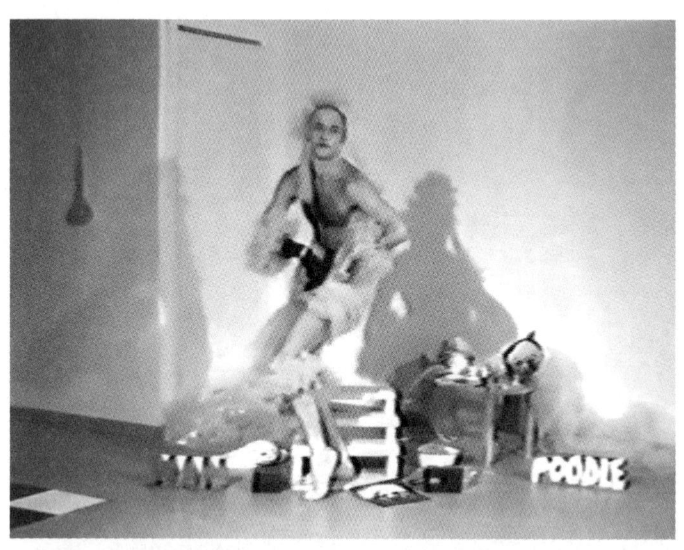

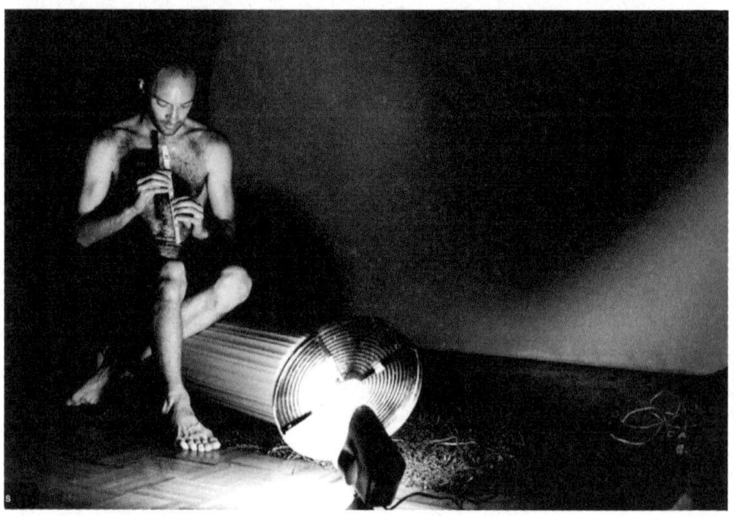

Top: *Poodle Theater*, video still, 1980; Bottom: *The Greek and French Arts*, Cincinnati, 1982.
Photo: Thom Middlebrook

22

# PETER HUTTINGER

*Artist, agriculture advocate, and art/book dealer*

Hudson and I both went to the University of Cincinnati. He graduated in 1977, the year before I came there, but we had mutual friends through the university community. After he got his MFA in painting he almost immediately started doing contemporary dance. So I kind of knew of him as a member of a troupe. He not only danced for Contemporary Dance Theater, but as I remember he was also very involved in its administration and development. It's still going today, and well respected in the region. Then at some point he injured his back, and had to quit dancing. That's when he transitioned to performance art. One of these things where you respond to what life gives you. Lance Kinz, who was then the director of the UC Fine Arts Gallery, introduced me to him when he did a performance there.

Hudson left CDT and started working for C.A.G.E. [*Cincinnati Artist Group Effort*]—people working independently in the community. A lot of people's careers and sensibilities were really shaped by the stuff that was going on at C.A.G.E. Hudson wasn't involved until maybe the second year but he became a crucial player. For a year or so he did all of the exhibition announcements for them, in a cut-and-paste style. They had an audio library, and I organized different audio projects that people could come in and listen to. Hudson organized performance events, including a number of his own pieces. He also collaborated a lot at the time with Nancy Henley, a very close friend of his. So I think all of this went straight into what he did later at Randolph Street Gallery when he moved to Chicago.

*In Cincinnati he had a project called Buzz Tone Outlet?*

Yes. That was an actual store, on Court Street. A really small storefront that he lived in. There was a storefront window with a backdrop and he'd stage different vignettes in it. Inside there was a counter and then a display area where different artists showed things. A lot of people did things at Buzz Tone Outlet. I remember Gregory Green did a hair shirt. But it was funny when you walked in. There was the shop, and there was the desk, and there was Hudson. And then there was a bedroom/studio apartment happening in view right behind him. I remember later over the years at Feature, Hudson always had his desk very visible in the same way. There was never a back room, so to speak. In fact I can remember talking once to an artist who showed at Feature about how it drove her crazy that any conversation you would have with him was completely visible. But I always thought it was brilliant.

Buzz Tone Outlet was in the heyday of answering machines, where people were fucking around with phone messages. Hudson did this extended narrative of messages on his machine, and it just blew up—what we would now call going viral. It was people constantly calling to hear these little updates of phone messages that he left. I'm not sure if there's any record of that, but they were totally hysterical. And then something happened where someone called and complained about the content. The phone company came down on him for it. But it was a pretty amazing thing while it lasted.

In 1980 or '81 C.A.G.E. did a 12" record in collaboration with the Composers Guild. One side was artist stuff and the other side was contemporary music. Hudson did a piece on that, based on the Buzz Tone Outlet thing. But it was more a sound textural piece using the keyboard on a push-tone phone. Anyway, for a long time personal friends just called him Buzz.

*Can you tell me about his performances?*

*Poodle Theater* was a piece that he did in Cincinnati. It was the beginning of the performances he was known for later that included props, signs, and nudity. He said that he had a reputation there, which became annoying. He also did an interesting piece at the Cincinnati Art Museum. It was a regional biennial and he dressed in an Uncle Sam hat and suspenders and stood on the front steps of the museum and handed out these postcards that had political texts which at that point were probably related to Reagan. I think the museum was kind of disappointed, because he had a reputation for performing nude. He was kind of like, "You want that? Well fuck you, you're not getting it." [*laughs*]

There's a Cincinnati newspaper interview with him around that time, where he expressed bitterness about the town. But also, I think you just kind of get burned out. Just in terms of the gay community in Cincinnati, we had the prestige of being the city that prosecuted the Mapplethorpe exhibition. So there was that kind of prevailing culture. He expressed to me that he wanted to go someplace where people's sexuality was not an issue. He was over it. He just wanted to be what he was. I mean, his work was widely accepted, and really loved by people in the community. The Ohio Arts Council funded projects by him, and they had great respect for him both as an arts administrator and as a performance artist. But in Cincinnati you're only going to go so far. He wanted to go where there was a larger gay community.

Hudson could be absolutely militant on certain things, but then there was also a high level of acceptance that he had for other people. I've seen that very, very few times in my life. That's what kind of drew me to him and why I had such great respect for him, because of that capacity.


## TONY TASSET

*Artist*

When I met Hudson in Cincinnati in the early '80s I wouldn't really say that we were friends, but I knew him to say hello. I went to this little art

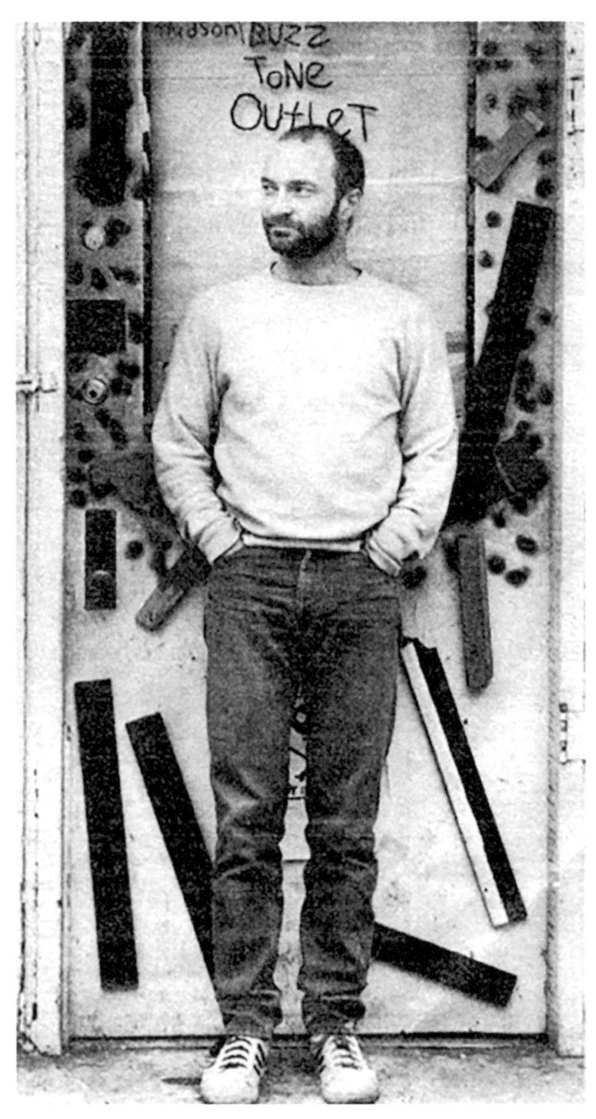



Cincinnati, 1982. Image from *Cincinnati Enquirer*. Photographer unknown

school, the Art Academy of Cincinnati. He taught performance, and was this character around town. He wore leopard skin stretch pants and he had a little more hair back then, which was fuchsia pink. He was also a member of C.A.G.E., an artists' coalition and non-profit space. I would see him around. I remember there was a bar downtown that once a week would turn into a new wave club, and they called it The Pit. I'd put my skinny tie on and we'd go dancing at The Pit, and Hudson was always there. He also had a little store. Not a gallery, but a store called Buzz Tone Outlet, which was mostly Xerox art. This was Cincinnati, so back then he stood out.

I don't want to say he was a star, but he was known as a successful artist in some ways. I definitely thought of him as someone who'd made it. He had a reputation as a performance artist, and those were great. I saw *Poodle Theater* and a couple of others. He was always naked. This was the time of Karen Finley and the Kipper Kids. There was a flavor to them and he was a part of that.

*You met again later in Chicago.*

Yes. My friends Judy Ledgerwood and Gregory Green were a year ahead of me in Cincinnati. They moved to Chicago to attend grad school at the School of the Art Institute, and I followed a year later. Hudson had already gotten there and then opened Feature [in 1984]. To us there was a question of, what did this gallery represent? In Chicago at that time the Hairy Who and the Imagists were still a strong influence. But in the bigger art world this was the Neo-Expressionist period—Schnabel and Salle, the Italians and the Germans. There were two galleries in Chicago that were showing more conceptual and minimalist work, Rhona Hoffman and Donald Young. They were great, but really more importers than exporters. Not many local artists. Hudson came along—and later [gallerist] Robbin Lockett—and he represented a shift that felt very dramatic. Our little crowd didn't want to be regionalists or even local artists; we were trying to be more global. Hudson had that vision. He didn't just put Chicago artists in a Chicago show, he would mix them with… I remember seeing Richard Prince there, Sherrie Levine.

Between my first and second year of grad school I was working at Rhona Hoffman Gallery. Rhona was smart and she saw that Hudson had this cool new gallery. Both of them decided to curate a summer show together—in the summer, galleries used to do group shows of people that weren't represented. I talked him into looking at my work, these framed surface pieces that I was making at SAIC and not only getting no response about from anyone, but just getting trashed at every crit. I had twelve or fifteen of these little pseudo-paintings wrapped in paper towels. [*laughs*] I opened them up and laid them on the floor, and right away Hudson was, "Yeah. I'll show this work." So I was in Hudson's half of this double show with Rhona. And then he decided to start showing me, and it was off to the races.

*Was Feature welcomed?*

Hmm. No, people were pissed at us. Just because they thought we were somehow rejecting… For instance, there was a big painting show that the Museum of Contemporary Art, Chicago, did called *The Spiritual in Art*. It was about modernism starting from a spiritual place, such as Kandinsky. There was a guy that was hanging around named Kevin Maginnis. He worked with Hudson to curate a counter-exhibition called *The Non-Spiritual in Art*. But there were all these painters that were opposed to it. There was a heated debate.

But collectors were interested in Feature. There were Chicago people that collected me early on. I'm only talking about six months ahead of others. There were the Stones—Donna and Howard Stone. Hudson brought them to me, and there were a few other local collectors. So I think he was definitely respected. I mean, Rhona recognized it.

It's a little ineffable to describe what his contribution was there as a dealer, but it was like working with an artist. We talked all the time. He was allergic to the hierarchy and hypocrisy of the art world, how money kind of screwed things up and had gotten out of hand. I felt the same thing. Also, thinking back, I had really early success. I was 25. I went from high school to undergrad to grad. And then my second year out I was showing in Europe, California, and New York. I was young and it kind of freaked me out. I had these fur pieces and he sold all of them. But then I sort of jettisoned the seduction and started making these empty vitrines. I sold a few, but in some ways I was sabotaging my career. I even started cutting into the walls, to put these boxes in. And Hudson never encouraged or discouraged me. We just talked about stuff, talked about the art. I feel like I had the freedom to really experiment and be an artist. And I've continued with that, continued over the years to change my work over and over again. In some ways that started with him.

Hudson would always show two artists, one in one room and one in the other. That was a kind of ethic with him. I remember in New York I did a show at Feature like that, with Charlie Ray. Charlie did the eight-foot-tall woman in one room, and in the other room I did this piece that was kind of a fake performance. I totally trashed the space. I had naked people running around. I had every trope of performance, from foodstuffs to dead fish to costumes. Hudson brought in a bunch of dildos that I threw around the room. It was dark. And then I cleaned it all up, and the actual show was just these documentations of the piece, these photographs. It was like being in a room where something had happened. I was thinking this morning that, wow, it was pretty great that he never gave me shit about any of those sort of dramatic changes that I continued to make. I've been doing this for a long time now. It's hard to assess every move that you make, like oh that worked or it didn't work. It's more like, well, certain things got me to this place and that place. And, I don't know, Feature just felt like a really, really fruitful time. Hudson was cool with it all. It was the one time as an artist that I felt

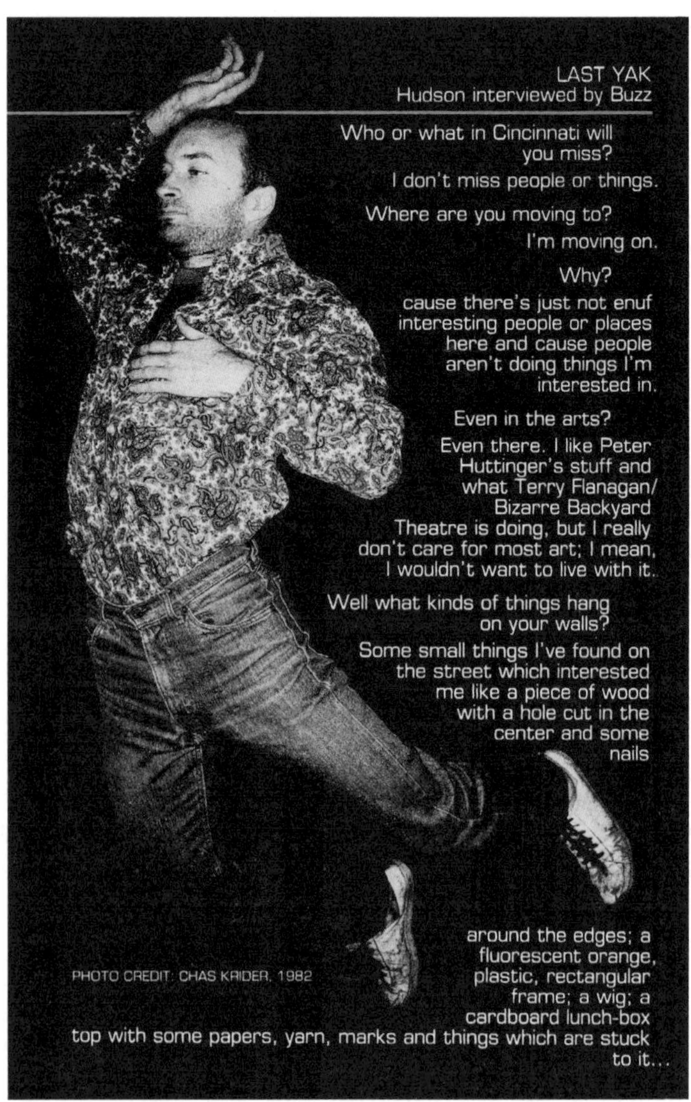


Hudson interviewed by 'Buzz' (Hudson), *Megazene*, 1982. Photo: Chas Krider

like I was cool. [*laughs*]

And then at one point he dumped almost all his artists! But even though I was one of those who was dumped, I continued to talk to him, and I continued to respect him, and I continued to go into the gallery and show him stuff. I made this wild kind of pornographic hot dog man sculpture, and I remember sending it to him and just wanting Hudson to see it. I always had a fantasy that I would show with him again, and I assumed that if he lived long enough I would have. Well, it was a great run while we had it.


## PETER TAUB

*Curator and arts administrator*

In the early '80s Nancy Forest Brown was the director of Randolph Street Gallery, and Hudson was the director of performance. I had the idea that he had come from Cincinnati to Chicago specifically for that job. Randolph Street Gallery started on Randolph, and was initially a place for artists who were part of a collective effort to show their own work. It started in 1979, and in 1982, I think, it moved to Milwaukee Avenue. My sense is that there was a quality of events and performances that attracted attendance. I think Hudson started working there in '82 or '83, and finished in 1984. I started in February 1986. So I knew of Hudson, but I didn't overlap with him.

The one performance I saw of his there was *Sophisticated Boom Boom,* which had its own mythology that preceded it. The piece had a kind of grand quality that was built out of very small, ephemeral or vernacular materials. He created a kind of one-man epic that was not done in the gallery's performance space, but was done in the white part of the gallery, the visual arts part of the gallery. He had this certainty and elegance about him even though he was doing stuff that had a kind of absurd and vulnerable side. He put himself out there without any kind of hesitation or apology. I felt like the work had an inner logic that he knew and you had to take as a leap of faith in order to get to the end.

I think that some of the artists he worked with at Feature had a performative sensibility. General Idea—and maybe this is my bias, as someone who looks at things through that lens—was in many ways doing performance-based work. Or even someone who is a visual artist, like David Robbins. It makes me wonder if Hudson's own practice in live arts influenced his sensibility at Feature, whether he recognized what certain artists were doing through his experience as somebody who used his own body in making work.

What I want to say about Hudson is that his phase at Randolph Street Gallery as an artist and a programmer was completely consistent with the identity of RSG. It may have begun as a place that allowed and promoted opportunities for member artists—a place to show work by people who were excluded from the commercial system—but it quickly became a place where any associated artists were there as organizers, as curators, as activists, but not as people who were showing their own work. Hudson's sensibility as an artist was reflected in how he developed programming. Working with artists from outside the Chicago area, like Karen Finley or Jack Smith, was consistent with what he followed through with at Feature. He employed his own sensibility, his own creative perspective as a maker to his work as a curator and administrator. Even after he left RSG and developed Feature he continued to stay in the field [of non-profit artist-run organizations]. He was even head of the board at the National Association of Artists Organizations for a number of years. That was an amazingly important organization, because for the first time there was a sense of perspective and place in the field. I found it completely unexpected—but I didn't recognize at the time how brilliant it was—that Hudson maintained his involvement in it while he was running Feature, a for-profit gallery.

# PAMELA GOLDEN

*Artist*

In 1981 I came to the School of the Art Institute for graduate school. I was in painting there, and at that time it was a very different kind of school, a much smaller place. I think in my group I was the only one who came from undergraduate school, and I was probably the only one from a state school as well. Everybody else was a bit older and from fancier places. It felt tough. But I had keys to the electronic music studio. I was doing a lot of music stuff. And SAIC is probably where I met Hudson. I know that the first time I laid eyes on him he was doing a performance, soon after he arrived.

In that period none of us went to art school thinking we were going to make money. It wasn't about being a careerist in any way. It was about trying new things and being part of the conversation. Phyllis Kind used to do these openings at her gallery with her ex-husband Josh. They were incredibly buoyant and generous to students, and they would have an open bar. I remember getting cocktails there, the kind I would never drink anywhere else. You were made to feel welcome, even though [those sorts of] galleries were selling pricey work. And we were also invited to the Museum of Contemporary Art, to their openings. Art wasn't a precious commodity. Everybody had jobs and also made art. Chicago felt like it was an easy place to be at the moment, and easy to have a studio you could make a mess in. We all had these enormous places, and they weren't hard to get. There was just empty real estate—people not using it.

The range of work that was happening in Chicago was anything you could imagine. There wasn't a house style, and there wasn't a judgement about it. You were exposed to a lot. And I think a lot of it was bouncing off of Reagan and what that brought up. And AIDS was the other thing, because right when I met Hudson was when the first person that I knew passed away. A flight attendant. It was pretty awful. And I remember one day that we both came in the gallery, and another friend had passed away. And we wept for a few days. We didn't even talk to each other, we just worked. There wasn't anything to say, it was just a sign of the times.

*You were the first employee of Feature?*

Hudson and I had been friends before that when he worked at Randolph Street Gallery. It was an incredible privilege that he asked me to work at Feature when it opened [*laughs*] because my secretarial skills were not great. My labelling of slides was not perfect.

He opened the gallery because he thought globally, and he was excited about work that was happening out there. He grabbed the moment as an opportunity to show things that nobody was seeing in Chicago. I remember that Charlie Ray show with the spinning black dot in the floor. [*Spinning Spot*] How nobody got injured is really quite amazing. But Hudson took a lot of risks, he was passionate about it.

I remember painting the gallery with him before it opened. And then I was the desk person. I was there a lot, I think half the week. He and I worked together at the beginning, and on Saturdays I was often there on my own. There wasn't a dress code or anything like that, but I wore a lot of bracelets, which always made him laugh. There kind of weren't any rules, and my role as far as what sort of office work I did kept decreasing the more inept he realized I was. But I was very interested in the work being shown. I'd read a lot about it, and he had me reading even more about it. So my job was basically to be informed. There was always new stuff coming in and a range of people to meet. People would send in slides all the time, and Hudson did actually look at them. He always wrote a small note, if I remember correctly. He was incredibly kind to do that. Some people were appropriate for the gallery and some people were appropriate for other galleries, and some people were just not really that interesting, or not there yet. I don't remember him being snide. He took it all very... he respected them. So they would get an envelope back. But he would be very diligent about that. And there would be stacks of things that would come in. Almost like fan mail.

Perfection was just his way of doing things. Yet he wouldn't expect that I would do it the same way, even though he would want it. Interesting. But he was absolutely precise about the installation and the care of the work. I know from later experience just how careful he was. Many times you get back things that are slightly damaged. That would never happen with Feature. I know that working at other galleries, you were running from the minute you got there and you did become careless. Hudson didn't rush things. Feature's business model reflected that. And part of working there was that you had to be responsible for looking after yourself physically. I attended a good yoga center, but I still felt at times I wasn't living up to that part of things.

The way the storage was treated was unusual too. It was done carefully, and all the work was precious, but you could take out works to show people any time. It was very accessible and easy to find. If people came in he wanted you to be able to show them what was there. It wasn't just for the collectors. He was so enthusiastic, it was contagious.

The other galleries in the building didn't necessarily have the same agenda but they all got on together. They would come and look too. The building was huge. It was a warehouse. Feature itself was not huge, but even people that I now know here in London remember it. They had gone to Chicago then and went to Feature. It was very much a moment. Part of that might have been the economy of the city, that you were able to do things. You could take some risks.

The openings there were absolutely packed, with a huge range of people. He did have collectors, although early on it was still that thing where they would only buy in New York. I remember one couple, they were going to buy a Jeff Koons in New York. They had seen it first at Hudson's, and they'd had a whole discussion with him. But there was something about

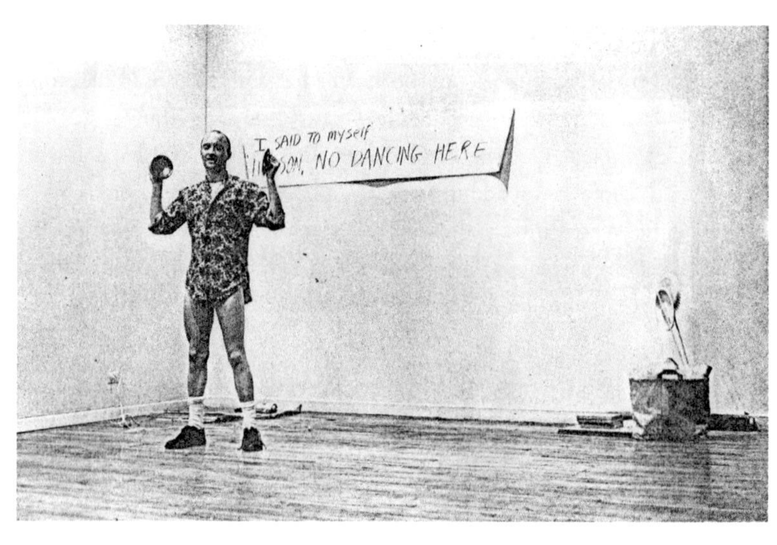


*World Without End Amen*, N.A.M.E. Gallery, Chicago, 1982. Photographer unknown

buying it in New York that had more caché then buying it in Chicago. Then there were the young collectors. That's when I met Clay Press and Greg Linn. They were probably at every opening and bought things from him. Ernestine Giesecke was another. And Richard Pollack. He had MS and would type out messages. So at the openings you'd get a piece of paper tape with one of his messages.

*You were showing there as well?*

Yes, and as an exhibiting artist at Feature myself, I thought Hudson was wonderful. He asked really tough questions, which was exactly what you wanted. [The artist/dealer business arrangement] was fluid. It wasn't going to be that he was going to take care of your needs forever. I think that was never in the cards, never part of his project or the gallery's. But I think the worst person he took care of in that way was himself. I don't think he was giving himself a proper salary. The artists were paid before he was.

In 1988 when he moved to New York and I would go there, I'd see if he had some time. He would always say that he was a bit busy, and would be kind of abrupt, but then "Meet me at this time and we'll have dinner." And I would think he was going to put aside an hour. But it wouldn't be an hour, it would be hours and hours. We'd go to a restaurant and by the time we'd leave I was ready to go to sleep. He would make the time.

After I moved to London he came a few times. His joke was that I would always take him to a park. And I did. We'd walk through all the parks, because they're all connected here. It was great. I felt like I had him on my own for a while. And he saw things that I hadn't noticed before.

He engaged with you very personally. He was listening, he was interested. And he was so funny. Oh my god. To the point where you're crying with laughter about completely silly things. He allowed that to happen. Rarely do you go into a gallery now where people are laughing.

# DARINKA NOVITOVIC CHASE

*Artist*

When I got out of school at SAIC in 1979 I didn't really know a lot of people in the art world. I wasn't too connected. But I joined West Hubbard Gallery, a co-op. Co-ops actually were a huge part of the scene there. N.A.M.E. Gallery, A.R.C., Filmmakers Cooperative. I was in a lot of group shows, of course. Chicago then was a bit behind the times. So in 1980 I curated a show called *Alter Ego* at West Hubbard. I included [younger Chicago artists] Jim Brinsfield, Angela, Michael Zieve, Deven Golden. It was a time of change, a lot of different kinds of work and was really fun. I remember there was *The Times Square Show* in New York, and there were some shows like that in Chicago. It was just in the air. Huge commercial spaces that were empty and that people would do gigantic shows in. One of my favorites that I was part of, was one that Billy Miller curated called *Possible Worlds*.

There was a lot of synchronicity. Dancing, performance art. It was just very easy and a lot of people were working. A pretty cooperative atmosphere. The music and the filmmaking and the art world were more intertwined. I remember years later Alex Katz telling me about the '60s, how it was so different because it was one art world in New York. The poets and the painters and the dancers, they all sort of knew each other and collaborated, and it was never about money yet. And actually, when Hudson opened Feature it still wasn't about that. It was still innocent in that everyone was making art and didn't think they would get rich.

I first saw Hudson at Randolph Street. He was doing a performance there and I went. He had his pants off and his top on, and he was acting like he was riding a horse across the stage, with his penis bouncing up and down. That's my very first memory of him. He was presenting interesting things there. And then he decided to open his own space. And honestly, I don't remember the conversation when he said, "Do you want to show with me?"

At first he had a one-year contract. One page of it was what the gallery was about, and the second page was what he was going to do for you and what he expected from you. Which was great, because it was very clear. He expected you to give him artwork, but it was more like, "Once I choose you, you give me what you want." He wasn't going to monitor it.

People signed up with the gallery, and it had a commitment to you and to your career. The contract said that you would have a one-person show, and that there would also always be a group show at the same time. So at that point, with so few artists represented by Hudson, you would always have some work on the walls. Hudson was an artist himself, and I felt comfortable with him. He was more of a contemporary to the younger artists. That's also what Mary Boone did, I think. They were all young.

I remember him coming to my loft for a studio visit. Although I don't recall the specific conversation, he was encouraging about my work, but he was also encouraging to me as a person. He was very… I won't say romantic, but he was very sweet.

*You felt like he understood the work?*

Absolutely. And also, he added to it. Because Hudson had a unique way of speaking. I think he got what I was doing, but also… I didn't always get everything that I was doing. He would see something that I wouldn't see. He saw a softness, for one.

So he had his first show, which was Richard Prince, and a group show that I was in. The opening was a Sunday in the afternoon, and everybody was really excited to be there. Some of the amazing things that had been bubbling up here and there… somebody had finally organized it. It was as if they'd said, "This is what it is, and we're going forward."

*Looking at the announcement now, there was remarkable variety. Your paint-ings, and work by Peter Huttinger, Rene Santos, Sarah Charlesworth, Jim Brinsfield, Sherrie Levine. And then the next month you had a solo show there.*

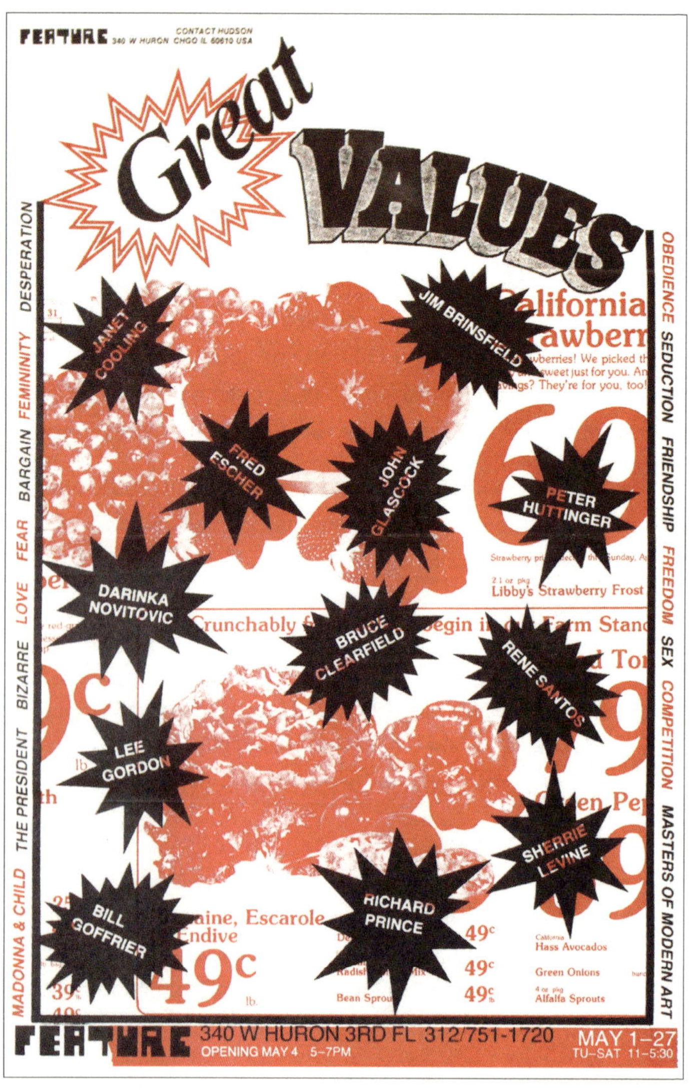


*Great Values* group exhibition announcement, Chicago, May 1984

I was honored. There were no reviews, but a lot of other artists loved it, and I was really happy. There weren't sales, but actually nobody had sales then. And I remember going through the show with Hudson once it was hung, and talking about the actual paintings. Which was really, really unusual in my experience until then. And then right after that I moved to New York.


## JAMES PEDERSEN

*Musician*


Feature opened on April Fool's Day, 1984. I was working for a gallery nearby that sold barn prints to dentists' offices and had a lot of free time to wander the neighborhood and meet the people who worked in the area. A friend of mine took me to Feature one day when I groused about only seeing twenty-ninth-generation Hairy Who wannabes or, as was popular at the time, Neo-Expressionism. My friend knew Hudson and introduced me. I don't remember the show now, but after that I went back for every one. The scene was pretty quiet in those days and Hudson was always ready to chat. I enjoyed him talking about the art he was showing and found that it was what I was needing to see then. This must have been late 1984 or early 1985. Part of my work at the time included framing, and he asked if I would frame some of those lovely Sherrie Levine appropriationist watercolors.

He was also on the NEA grant review panels at the time and had to go to Washington every other weekend. My friend Pam Golden usually gallery-sat when he was away. There must have been a week where she couldn't do it and he asked me instead. Maybe he started asking me more often because I didn't change the TV channel on Hirsch Perlman's sculpture! But I gradually worked more often there. I began helping out with installations and sending out monthly mailings, and little by little I was becoming his assistant.

*What work did you most appreciate in those early years?*

Peter Huttinger was probably the first artist that I glommed onto. There was always the photography, too. You know, Louise Lawler with a photograph of a styrofoam cup. That was very strange to me. The Rene Santos photos off the television. My favorite art era is the Gordon Matta-Clark and Carl Andre sort of thing, so I really did appreciate the cool aesthetic these things were throwing off.

*Would you say there was a mission?*

Hudson didn't talk so much about what the gallery's mission was. He had this reputation that everything [he showed] was super conceptual, but he was from the get-go fairly pluralistic and that kept on through the whole project. He was always going to New York to do studio visits. I understood that he was really turned on to the Pictures people. But there were also artists like Peter Huttinger, Jim Brinsfield, and Darinka Novitovic who were not in that aesthetic frame.

None of those people were represented by big galleries in New York at that time. Instead it was 303, International With Monument, Cable, Nature Morte, Metro Pictures… these were all still kind of punky East Village galleries. I'm guessing they saw Feature as just the western outpost of the East Village. So he was talking to gallery people like Lisa Spellman, Peter Nagy. That whole scene was like, hey, let's open a gallery. As ambitious as all those people were, it was still a fly-by-night thing at the time.

Hudson was also looking west. He had Jim Isermann, Charlie Ray, Raymond Pettibon, Jim Shaw. And he had the midwest, the Chicago people. He wanted to promote artists from Chicago that were not of the previous mold. So there was a little bit of proselytizing for a more pluralist look at art. His aesthetic was more about the non-profit galleries. He could be scathing about the Phyllis Kind stable. But he could also say, "That's a really beautiful Ed Paschke painting" every once in a while. I think of him being more of a… like I know he was friends with Rhona [Hoffman]. He appreciated Donald Young's gallery also. He and Rhona did an invitational, where he put a show together for her and she put a show together for him. So I wonder how much his public persona was in reaction to the bewilderment and hostility of the rest of the art world. A defense mechanism.

*Who did visit Feature in those early years?*

There was not a lot of foot traffic because it was on the third floor, way in the back of the building. People didn't stumble upon it. During the week you'd get some people, but I got a lot of reading done! A lot of people came on Saturdays. They'd get out the Gallery Guide and follow the map. It was a Louis Sullivan warehouse building, by the way. And right after we moved to New York in 1988 it burned to the ground.

He had the eight or so Chicago artists that he represented, so people would come to see their shows. And there were other locals in Feature shows too. People like Anita David and Mitchell Kane. A lot of them eventually would either land in Robbin Lockett's gallery or stick around the not-for-profit world. And then everyone else who wasn't trying to get into Phyllis Kind was trying to get into Rhona Hoffman or Donald Young. But Rhona and Donald weren't interested in the local talent, mostly.

*Who was collecting?*

Ernestine Giesecke supported him. Elizabeth Byrd Loyd for the Allen Art Museum at Oberlin. Richard Sander bought photographs. I remember during the Chicago Art Fair all these New York people coming in and saying, "Show me some Richard Prince photos." I don't know that he sold a lot of work. Linda Horn bought a few things. Jerry Elliot. The Progressive Insurance Corporation would buy stuff. They had a solid set-aside budget. Peter Lewis was the chairman, and his ex-wife Toby would come through at least two or three times a year and pick things out to put in people's offices.

But Hudson couldn't crack the top tier of Chicago collectors, which I think was another layer of frustration he had. The people who would later buy these artists from Rhona and Donald wouldn't buy them from him.

*I remember interesting evening events at Feature.*

Hudson wanted to do a multi-discipline thing. He had readings and video screenings. He showed Todd Haynes' *Superstar*, for instance. William Wegman videos. When he did his response to the Museum of Contemporary Art's *The Spiritual in Art* show in 1987, he allowed me to curate a music night. Another time I was working with the Loop Group, and he let me use the gallery space for a concert.

I didn't get involved in installations at first, because they were small shows and mostly it was just Hudson banging nails into a wall. The space was small and there would be seven photographs and three paintings or something like that. Charlie Ray's first piece that I remember was *How a Table Works*. That just came in a big crate. You didn't have to… [*laughs*] didn't have to kill anybody, unlike his *Spinning Spot*, where we had to build up the floor. That piece kind of terrified me. I don't know how many RPMs it was moving, but somebody said if it came loose it would destroy everything in its path. Someone eventually did step on it. The guy was wearing, like, Nikes. He accidentally put his foot on it, didn't even press down, and it must have been for only a fraction of a second, but it just melted the bottom of his shoe away. We had to turn the thing off, sand the rubber off, and repaint it. Also, the motor was loud. Other people in the building were asking, "What the hell is this noise?" And I remember still painting the fake floor for it while the opening was going on. That was always one of my pet peeves. It would happen fairly often in the beginning that I was still installing when the opening started, and Hudson would let people in. I'm on the floor installing something and people are walking around spilling juice and beer on my hands.

*After the first few years the New York artists stopped showing at Feature.*

They were making waves. The galleries they were showing with in New

York were becoming hot. Or they were just moving on. Richard Prince moved on to Barbara Gladstone. It was a combination, actually, of those artists moving up in the world and Hudson finding a new group of Chicago people. Then I think his mission shifted a little bit to be more of a showcase for the Chicago crowd. The last year in Chicago, especially, was about showing Chicagoans like Hirsch Perlman, Jeanne Dunning, Tony Tasset.

In 1988, after working with Hudson on an ad hoc basis for two to three years, he took me on full-time. But that was short-lived as Feature lost its lease a few months later. Together we looked around at spaces and almost signed on an interesting one near Halsted and North Avenue, but he decided that the numbers weren't that far from what he'd be paying in New York, and since he felt Chicago wasn't supporting his venture, he decided to pull up stakes and head east. I had been unhappy with Chicago as well, and at some point I asked if I could work for him in New York. He was very happy about that. Hudson and I had similar senses of humor, similar personalities, and he appreciated my attention to detail and my thoroughness and professionalism.

I had left my other gallery job by then and was working a few shifts at a nearby restaurant. Feature had no air conditioning, and I used to go to the restaurant where they'd let me take a garbage bag full of ice back to the gallery. Hudson and I would take off our shoes and stick our feet in buckets full of ice water to be able to work. The closing up of the Chicago space happened in early summer during one of Chicago's notorious heat waves. I remember almost passing out in the freight elevator.

*And New York's gain was Chicago's rather big loss.*

In Chicago Hudson was the nucleus of a really great group of people: artists, collectors, hangers-on, and just plain interesting humans. Yes, there was a great sense of loss when he left, and a social vacuum resulted along with that. There were many farewell parties for us, from North Avenue to Gary, Indiana.

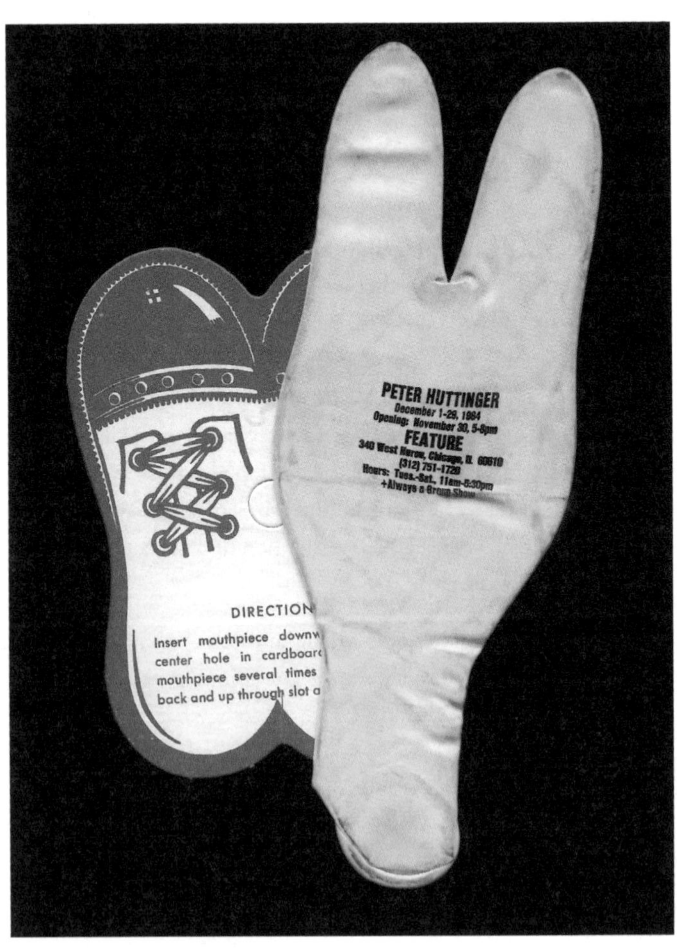


Peter Huttinger exhibition announcement (balloon and cardboard stand), Chicago, December 1984

Yes. I came out a few months later but Hudson did fly me in to install the first show and help set up the gallery. For the opening a lot of Chicago people came out and a lot of the New York people who supported Hudson showed up as well. The Broome Street space was really pretty and was always my favorite of them all. And it had air conditioning.

Hudson had lost his backer and he was unable to pay me full time. I got a waiter job in the neighborhood to help pay the bills. Nancy Shaver took me under her wing and got me set up at Dia and called me quite a bit to sub for her when she needed a day off. I loved sitting in *The Broken Kilometer.* In the meantime, I worked nearly full time for Hudson anyway and got some nice deals on artwork in consideration.

*Did you have a title there?*

During the majority of my working career at Feature, I was its only employee. I didn't really have a title besides the informal one of "Hudson's assistant." I pretty much did everything. Besides opening and closing the gallery every day, I answered phones, cleaned windows, labeled slides, managed artists' bios and kept an inventory of their work, made up press packets, combed publications for reviews, created and managed archives of the gallery's activities, copyedited and proofread publications—including Feature's magazine *Farm* [*an occasional publication highlighting the work of the gallery's artists and others, as well as writing and found imagery*]— installed exhibitions, did most of the packing and shipping, kept inventory of art on the premises and out on loan, ran errands, assisted with photo shoots, learned how to get art through US customs, along with all the other things that must be done to keep a New York gallery in business.

He had many people come in over the years to help with mailings, office stuff, and installations and a great many of them were fun to have around. Jimi Dams came along in the mid-'90s and ended up taking over some of my more clerical chores. Jimi and I became great friends right away, and I still love him dearly and have fond memories of the fun we would have together when "the cat was away." After we moved to Chelsea, we had a few others working part time and I was pretty much devoting my time to the tasks of a registrar: keeping inventory, packing and shipping, artists' bios, and press packets. I also continued to oversee installations. When an artist was present for the installation, they had pretty much complete say-so over the placement of their work. But many asked my advice, as well as the advice, of course, of Hudson. Much more fun for me were group shows when Hudson would allow me to install as I liked. Sometimes we would work together and that was fun too. But he really trusted my eye and most of the group exhibitions were laid out by me.

*How long were you at the gallery?*

I continued working at Feature until 2001. Hudson had changed quite a bit over the years, and we were often at loggerheads by then. My health had had its ups and downs and the physical aspects of installing and packing artworks were getting to be hard for me to manage. After my hospitalization for cancer that March, I tried to keep working during my chemo treatments. It seemed to me that Hudson had difficulty with this situation as I was not always feeling well enough to come in when we had agreed. He was always able to rely on me, and I was always willing to "be there" for him, but this change in dynamic proved too much for either of us to overcome. It seemed a good time to end a relationship that had lasted over sixteen years.

## CHARLES RAY

*Artist*

In the early '80s I was living in Los Angeles and Feature was in Chicago. I didn't know Hudson or of the program he was developing at Feature, but he wrote me a letter telling me that for a number of years he was following my work and would like to exhibit it.

*Had he seen it in person?*

I think he had found the images from when I was doing the performance pieces. That's what he called the sculptures that my body was in, from the early '80s. But I'd stopped doing them maybe a year before his letter came. When I wrote back, I sent him some slides of newer sculptures. He was interested in meeting and talking.

*Were you showing with Burnett Miller in L.A. previous to that?*

I would say around the same time. The first thing I showed with Burnett was *Ink Box*. And the first thing I showed with Hudson was *How a Table Works*, although it comes earlier in the chronology than *Ink Box*. I would almost say it was Feature first, or at least it was his interest first.

*How different were the galleries?*

Burnett and Hudson were both individual people, but in really different ways. Burnett put on an air of being blue chip. Whether he was or not, I don't know. He had a big kind of low-ceilings-warehouse-y space. You went in and you kind of thought you were in Germany or something. Big cement floors and cement ceiling. But they were both enthusiastic in different ways. Burnett was a little like a painting, and Hudson felt a bit more within my work stream. Burnett was interested, came to the studio. Hudson lived further, so didn't come as much.

Hudson in his own strange way was a real connoisseur. Whereas someone like Burnett liked black. [*laughs*] Like a black hat, or like my *Ink Box*, because it was, you know, black. It's not that Hudson didn't show some of my ink pieces and the tub with black dye. But he was more intrigued by the inside of something flipped out. Like you could take a cat and turn it inside out. He would have that as a pet. I don't quite mean it. It was more how he could talk about an idea, and turn it inside out.

You know, for some years I talked to Hudson almost every day on the telephone, or every night. He was always working late at night. It was just one of those things that I grew through. I think we both thought of each other as friends, but we really weren't. We were close, but we weren't each other's friend because we were dealing not in our souls, but in art. I had my art, he had his gallery. We were interested in talking about art and thinking about it. So when I say we weren't friends, we… it was even better. It was more real than being a friend. Why should we be friends? We were doing this other thing that maybe we couldn't do with a friend. It was different things that were driving the association. But we had a falling out. Hudson had a half-life, at least with me. I always kind of thought that that was okay, though. It wasn't that I outgrew him or he outgrew me, or we changed in terms of our interest. It was just kind of a financial equation. I started doing bigger things and having other galleries coming into play with funding for projects. And, you know, Hudson was a little bit of a renegade. Funding had an almost bad connotation to him. And, I think, bad experiences in terms of other artists he showed when they were younger.

I wouldn't even say it was about financial opportunities, more like cultural opportunities. Not in terms of museums or anything, but looking into the matrix of one's place and time. That quality of expense of an object was part of that mix. Leaving a restaurant at night and seeing an expensive car parked in front and what all those connotations are, how it's made and who made it, who's driving, culturally why, and blah blah blah. Bringing those into one's art. He would kill me hearing me say it today, but he didn't have the means to support some of the things that I, and perhaps some of his other artists, wanted to do.

And you know, Hudson said, "I don't do dinners." Meaning that he didn't mess around with dinners with collectors at night and this and that, and do all the openings kind of stuff.

*There seem to be few art dealers that shared his priorities to the work itself, both then and now. In what ways do you think his approach was successful?*

I would like to change your question, and perhaps that's also my answer. I would change the first part of the first sentence to: "There seem to be a few art dealers that shared Hudson's priorities to the work itself, both then and now." I insert the "a" in front of "few" not because Hudson wasn't unique, but because he was truly counter-cultural. And to be counter-cultural takes a society rather than an individual. Hudson set his own agenda concerning the art he promoted but he spoke a common language of both the artists and collectors he involved himself with.

Before this conversation you asked me if I could expand on a thought from his obituary that I wrote for *Artforum*, that it was incredibly valuable for artists, and also collectors and viewers, to find the courage to create a relationship to what they made, looked at, and collected. I guess that's what I mean, working with Hudson as an artist or a collector was a rich experience. Hudson's role was less stable than a traditional art dealer's. If he seemed to be both the collector and the artist, it was because he had a natural ability to share his sensibility. He wasn't afraid to express his likes and dislikes. This never seemed to be a matter of taste, nor of his thinking alone, but rather a cultural thought. He understood our place and time, and our ways of thinking and speaking.

All the work that I showed with him was embedded in my sensibility and Feature's sensibility, just like Feature's sensibility was embedded in me. Hudson and Feature and my work were kind of intertwined. As weird as Burnett was, when I went into the gallery it was a little bit more formal. I'm in my gallery. Whereas at Feature, I was in Feature. I was very comfortable coming in and going out and having weird speculations with him and stuff. And I always thought he was available mentally.

*Did you find the same thing post-Hudson with other dealers?*

Hudson was unusual for only one reason—that he was Hudson, you know? [*laughs*] And if he didn't have a gallery, he would've still been unusual. So for me to put it in the context of "Was there another?," that's why I had to put the "a" in front of "few" in what I said earlier. I'm friends with and have deep relationships with other galleries. But Hudson was a really unusual guy. And at the same time, for me, what was unusual about him wasn't really special. It was just Hudson. Like, he did all those weird things with those weird doctors. He was swearing by that stuff, and you would just go, oh man. And all the street sex talk. Like a lot of things, he just made it very kind of accessible to himself. It was like the color of the shirt he was wearing on any particular day. It wasn't heavy to him or anything.

*Someone else said they thought that he simply did everything for himself. That he had realized if you maintain a singular point of view in looking at art and showing it, not trying to please any criteria other than your own, you bring a lot more people along.*

You know, I was thinking of this: I knew he had to move to New York, but there was something different about Hudson in Chicago. I worked with him many years in New York and showed many great pieces with him there. But my memories are that there was something freer in Chicago somehow. In New York he never got a chip on his shoulder, but there was always this kind of struggle with other dealers. In Chicago it seemed a little bit freer, even with people like Prince, Koons, and myself showing with him. In New York it was really important, but it just didn't have that kind of… That was actually part of our falling out, my working with more people, and all the dealers don't really like each other that much, especially if you're working with more than one.

*Once Feature was in New York, I think he knew he had to really present something and maintain that level. Feature was popular with interesting and hip people, but that's hardly the New York art world in total. So I think there was always a little tension, to try harder.*

Yeah. And a beautiful thing about New York—I never talked about it with Hudson—but it's like he brought Chicago with him. There was just something about the way he set up those galleries that seemed kind of awkward, with the racks sort of in the main space almost. And it wasn't architecturally like the big Barbara Gladstone/Gagosian drywall/glass door kind of thing. The way it was genetically laid out in Chicago, it always stayed that way. I liked it.

I was thinking about this today: there was a reverberation back of scale. Feature always had a certain, I wouldn't say modest, but a particular scale, and that reverberated back into my work. I did a lot of table size pieces and figurative work then. I never a hundred percent liked the proportions of the Burnett space because of the low ceiling. It was a little bit oppressive. Feature's weren't much higher, but it always had a more kind of art domestic space to it. It was in a certain sense less minimalist, more post-minimalist. It was almost like a studio space, but a clean room in a studio or something. And it was a different kind of light in his space. It was just… warm would be the wrong word, but it was warmer. It was never corporate.

I do think if Hudson wanted to have a big warehouse type gallery, he would have. Or he could have easily been a director of an alternative space. He could have done the New Museum or something else if he wanted to. He was almost that way at Feature. It was sort of like a kunsthalle, like sales weren't important. He wanted to sell things, and he was irritated when someone else sold what he had showed first, but the primary concern was always the show, the art.

Eventually I was showing with more people. But I'm basically a one-gallery person, and even though I had other galleries, Feature was kind of *my* gallery. You know, with our big falling out it never turned nasty, really, I just didn't go in or he didn't call. We just stopped talking. But with time, I would go to the gallery once in a while. When he was down in the Canal

Street area, I would go in. He always seemed happy, but sometimes he'd say, "You know, you're making me really nervous being here." "Okay, I'll go." [*laughs*] That was pure too.

*It's been brought up how present Hudson could be, easy to relate to, but while clearly keeping a side of himself that was intangible and remote. It's usually remarked on as a positive quality, by the way.*

Yeah. It was a distance. I mean, it was easy for me because I guess I'm a distant person to other people anyway. So that kind of distance Hudson maintained where you could have a kind of wild time with him or dinner with him or something like that, while there was still a remoteness that I had with him, and he had with me. He made it seem friendly.

*So, could there be a modern-day version of Hudson as an art dealer?*

No way. No, not at all in these times. And that's beautiful. But there's just no way that I could see it. I guess *he* could still survive. I mean, he could still be here because he could be holding onto his rope, tied to where he began. But somebody now would have to tie the rope somewhere here. It would never be the same, you know? It would just be a parody of him.

## KAY ROSEN

*Artist*

I studied linguistics, so I was kind of a newcomer to the art world. I didn't come up through the normal ranks. I went to school in New Orleans, at Tulane, and I got my degree at Northwestern. Then I taught. But I got tired of academia. I was still interested in language, but I became more interested in the visual aspect of it. How the things I saw as interesting in linguistics needed to be expressed visually, with color or scale or font style. So I segued into that in the late '60s, and I just kind of worked on my own. In the late '70s I hooked up with a gallery in New York that in a previous life had been a kind of conceptual gallery on the Upper East Side. I showed there from about 1978 to '82, and then I was sort of looking around. And that's when I happened to read some little tidbit about Hudson, who was about to open a gallery in Chicago. He had been the performance curator at Randolph Street Gallery, and I think I had met him there. When Feature opened I stopped in, and honestly I cannot remember how it happened that I joined the gallery. [*laughs*] I don't even know if it was anything very official. I do remember that he was wearing a white t-shirt. He was very Hudson, very smiley.

*What was your impression of the gallery in those days?*

I'm not sure I quite understood at the beginning what Hudson's program was, or what he was trying to do. But Feature just felt like an opportunity for opening up the system.

*What was your first show?*

I think it was in 1984, a two-person show with Gregory Green. I showed a big installation, *No Noose Is Good Noose*. I wasn't formally with Feature then, so it was a test.

*Looking at the list of exhibitions, you were in almost every group show and had a few solos as well. I remember a show with you and Jamie Reid, who designed the Sex Pistols' graphics.*

Yes! There was also one with Jim Isermann. It was exciting then. The thing with Hudson… when he would call with good news, about a show or a sale or a this or a that, I felt like a girl being asked out on my first date. [*laughs*] It was like a thrill, you know what I mean? It was really fun.

*You opened Feature when it moved to New York in 1988.*

*The Ed Paintings* series. But you know what we did, it was so stupid. We had them for sale individually. But then I said to Hudson, "You know, I kind of think these should have been a set." Because they were a narrative.

Well, he had already sold two and I had traded one other, but he made arrangements to bring them back together. One woman agreed and took something else. The other fellow who had bought one would only give it up if I agreed to paint him another one, which I did. And the trade agreed to give it up and take something else as well. I was really grateful to Hudson for doing that, because it was kind of a pain in the ass.

*What stands out in your memory about that time?*

It was an unusual format. There were almost always two artists doing separate shows in the gallery. It was like Hudson didn't want to give anyone too much limelight. But that included himself. There was this kind of democratic thing about it, although I think that he was the star in a way. And I really couldn't tell you if it was intentional. Hudson kept an iron hand on how things functioned, but he was very accessible. You could talk to him about things without huge formality. I felt like he didn't play by the same rules as a lot of other galleries. Most were hype-y, and if something happened for one of their artists they really played it up. Hudson did the opposite. I remember when *Artforum* came out and I was on the cover, an article by Judith Kirshner. They sort of hid it behind the desk! There wasn't email then and the kind of distribution of information that we have now, but it was still withheld. It was frustrating. I think it was frustrating for a lot of the artists. I'm not sure the reason for this. I never asked. But he was like the strict father. I know he was happy about all these things that happened, but he never seemed to want to share it. So I thought that was unusual.

*Was business conducted in a different way? Percentages on sales?*

No, that seemed the same as anywhere else. It was the way he did advertising and promotion that was different. I remember once talking with him about how radically the gallery was run, and him saying, "That's why I do everything so quietly."

*In such a revisionist gallery, did you feel that you had a clear understanding of your business relationship with Hudson?*

Oh yes. At some point—and I'm not sure when it was, probably the real early '90s—he sent out a long list of what he thought the artists' obligations were, and what his were. I may still have a copy of it somewhere.

You know, looking back after I've had a succession of other galleries, I realize that they all have their quirks. Their own kinds of challenges. I envy artists who've had stable relationships with theirs, because I've gone through a succession and not always by choice. Several times they closed. In fact that seems to be the main reason. With Hudson, he changed the format. That was fine, really. At that point in '93, I think we were all about ready to have a revolt or something. Maybe he caught wind of it? I don't know. But he beat us to the punch.

*What made people pay so much attention to this small gallery?*

It was his eye, which was phenomenal, and his commitment to that. He really couldn't be corrupted, I don't think. He could be swayed a little bit [*laughs*]. I remember when he tried to sell those Jeff Koons basketballs. I think they were, like, $2,500. Can you imagine? And I think Donald Young, out of mercy, finally bought one. [*laughs*]

*He took such delight in language, and was especially attracted to your work for that reason.*

I always felt like he really appreciated what I was doing. But that was a thread that went through all of Hudson's artists, that kind of sense of humor. I don't remember actually talking that much about it, but part of the thrill of talking to him was that I knew he got it, and he knew I knew. As late as 2012 or 2013, I got the sweetest letter from him after he saw a show of mine at Sikkema Jenkins. It was just so beautiful, I treasure it. He talked a lot about the work, color and language, you know. He really understood it.

# STEVE LAFRENIERE

*Writer and designer*

I first laid eyes on Hudson in Chicago. I'm pretty sure it was 1982. I kept noticing this bald fellow at gallery openings, always in white jeans and a white t-shirt, and he had such an interesting face. Hard to miss. I noticed that he would ignore the wine and chatter, and sidle up to each piece and sort of stare it down. Then he'd be gone. One night I went to something at Randolph Street Gallery, and he was working at the door. Afterwards on my way out he kind of cruised me and I stopped and we talked a minute. It turned out he was the performance director there. I gave him my phone number and after that it fell into place pretty quickly, somewhere in the spectrum between friends and lovers over the next few years. Which is always an interesting spectrum.

*What kind of presence did he have in Chicago in those years before Feature?*

Well, first of all, he got everywhere on a yellow ten-speed bike. Even in winter, and in Chicago that's brutal. Warmer weather he never wore a shirt, so you'd see this wiry skinhead flying by at top speed in just white Levis and white leather sneakers that were kind of all mud-splattered. His physique was tight and, cliché that it is, he moved like a cat. He had an exercise routine that included a number of moves from his past as a dancer. There was a nagging leg injury from that time and he was trying to work through it with a naprapath, as well as Ayurvedic medicine, of which he was very much a devotee. Also a strict vegetarian. I remember one time him telling me that he'd never tasted a Coke before. If anybody else had said this, I'd have called bullshit. I think it's also important to know that he meditated twice a day. Transcendental Meditation. In over thirty years I don't think he mentioned to me a day that he skipped it.

He had a reputation for being intensely hardworking, and for his unre-pentant queerness. Hudson could be kind of startling in the things he'd talk about openly, his exploits. But that was rolled into everything else he would be saying. He was friendly and engaging, and came across as supremely honest. He told you precisely what he thought. Which could be harsh. To be honest, I'd never known anyone quite like this.

*Can you talk a bit about his performance work then?*

I'm probably not the one to analyze that body of work, which was fairly extensive, but I can flesh out some things. From what I understood, in Cincinnati in the late '70s Hudson was an avant-garde dancer who'd sort of edged into performance art. By the time I was seeing him in Chicago a few years later what he was doing seemed to me in the chaotic lineage of Allan Kaprow in the '60s. Solo work but with quite a few props around him, and many things going on. He was using recorded sound and text quite a bit. There were handwritten signs and loud verbal declarations. He blended all this with dance moves and usually a pretty far-ranging and startling soundtrack of music and sound samples. He'd start and stop them on a boombox. The props were simple and homemade. Actually, a lot of times he built or drew them during the performance itself.

*Subject matter?*

He dealt with politics, sex, history, art, culture, all the stuff that was on his mind or just in the air at the time. I've always thought of it as a kind of therapy for himself and the audience. Working out contradictions or inner conflicts versus observations of the outside world. Very funny a lot of the time. And often naked, which was appropriate. He got known for it.

The shows were pretty anticipated. There were lines to get in. Chicago was and is a theater town. In the '80s there were loads of actors, monologists, performance artists, improv groups, storefront theaters. He came to the right place, was prepared, and became well-regarded.

*In addition to this and heading the performance program at the non-profit Randolph Street Gallery, he was also heading the board at the National Asso-*

*ciation of Artists Organizations [NAAO].*

Yes, all of those. He was super engaged.

*And suddenly in 1984 he decided to open Feature, a for-profit gallery?*

I wouldn't say suddenly. He had talked about it to me for quite a while. The committee model of the non-profits that he'd been working with was tiring him. You have to remember that he was so disciplined in his approach to work—I used to to call him the Art Marine. He was also far-reaching in his sympathies, and much that interested him was not being shown in Chicago. Committees always lag. Hudson wanted to move forward more quickly, and at his own discretion. Hence... Feature. His friend Bill Olander in New York was also an influence on the decision to do it, introducing him to a coterie of younger artists that he recognized as important and that he strongly wanted to promote.

*How do you remember the Chicago Feature?*

It was in an immense warehouse building, and you had to wind your way up stairs and through long corridors to get up to the gallery itself. Inside, it was an average-sized white box with high ceilings. It opened on April Fool's Day 1984 and soon enough became a popular art haunt by word-of-mouth, a destination. The first year or two was especially exciting. I don't think Chicago was quite prepared. [*laughs*] Charlie Ray showed the bathtub filled with black dye and had his *Spinning Spot* piece embedded in the floor. Koons showed the equilibrium tank with basketballs and Nike posters. There was Richard Prince's joke series. Challenging young Chicago artists too. Black light paintings by Darinka Novitovic Chase and Tony Tasset's various objects and installations. These sublime Richard Rezac sculptures. Startling and hilarious word paintings by Kay Rosen. I remember that at her first show a friend told Hudson he felt like he was on acid and could no longer understand language. Hudson liked this. "Success!"

Feature also did readings. Dennis Cooper was flown in, and Gary Indiana

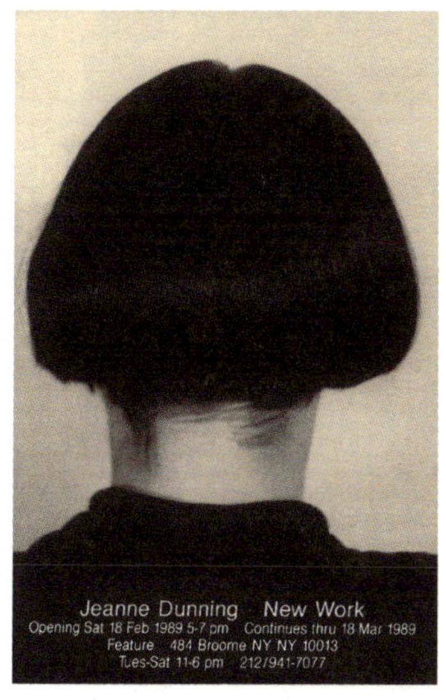


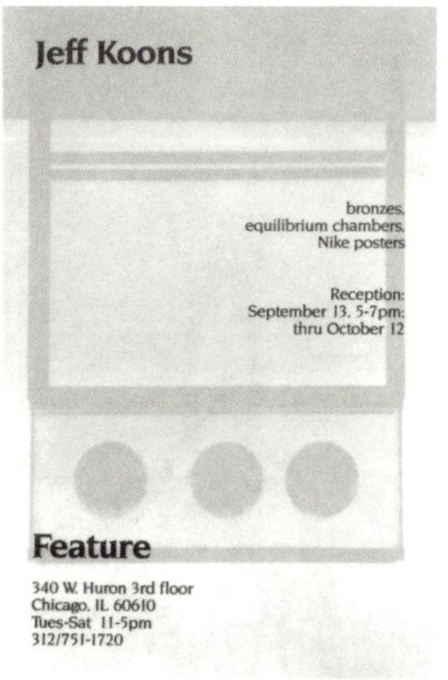


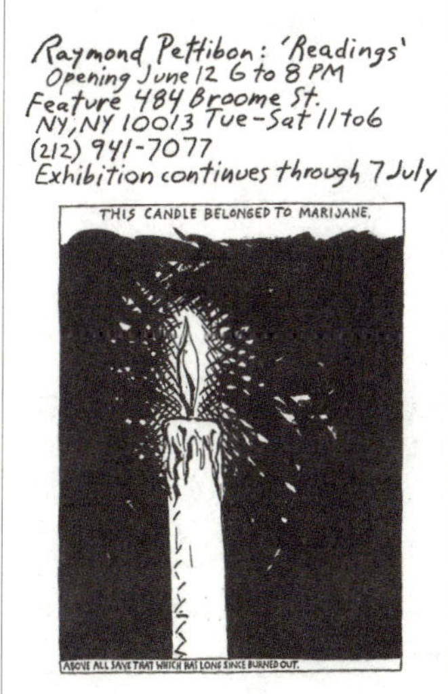


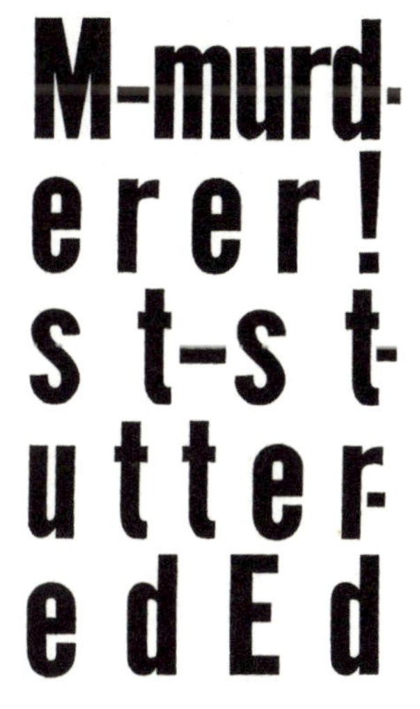


Clockwise: Jeanne Dunning, February 1989; Jeff Koons, September 1985; Kay Rosen, October 1988; Raymond Pettibon, June 1990 (All New York City, except Jeff Koons)

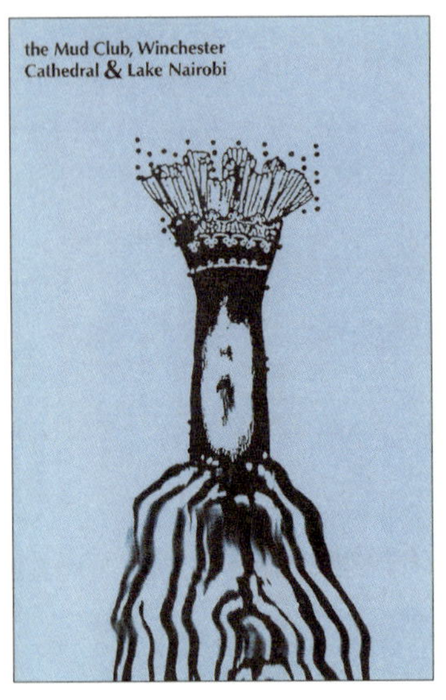


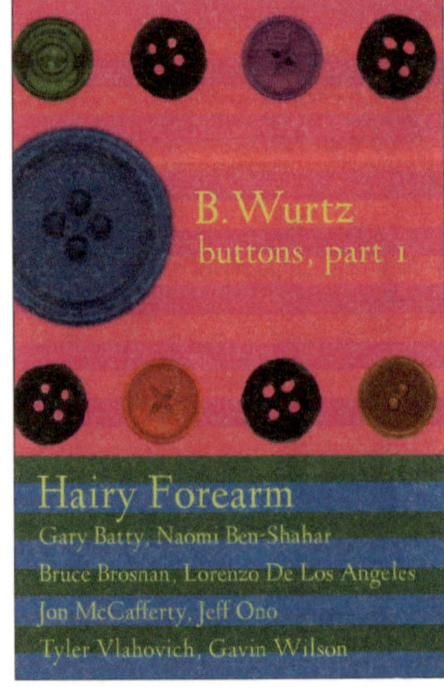


**Q & D**

Q: *Rumor has it you now claim to be making comedy, not art.*

D: So I assert, at times humorlessly.

Q: *Whence the change?*

D: It's only a shift in emphasis, but it makes all the difference in the world. Back when I was consciously identifying myself as an artist, there was a comic aspect to the work which many people misread as cynicism. I never understood what they meant by the accusation, because I always felt entirely sincere, but I'll admit it took a while for me to understand the exact object of my sincerity. At a certain point I understood that I was really performing a kind of conceptual, concrete comedy, not a conceptual art. Rather, I stopped being concerned about whether or not it was actually art at all. I freed myself to behave as I was interested to behave.

Q: *Gee, you're right, you are humorless about it.*

D: Sorry.

Q: *If you're practicing a conceptual comedy rather than a conceptual art, why do you continue to exhibit in art galleries?*

D: Is there any other institution at present that would accept the objects and images produced by such an endeavor? Anyway, galleries are extremely useful institutions and are subjected to too much disparagement by young artists. These days it isn't so difficult to find gallerists who are actively interested in testing the nature of their own endeavor, and they welcome someone like me.

Q: *What do galleries allow?*

D: That's a straw man's question.

Q: *I'm a straw man.*

D: True. I use galleries for two reasons. One: Only by engaging the gallery can one access the non-fiction integrity they frame —

# JAMES WELLING

## Selected

Clockwise: *the Mud Club, Winchester Cathedral & Lake Nairobi,* October 1992; David Robbins, November 1991; B. Wurtz and *Hairy Forearm,* January 2000; James Welling, April 1988 (All New York City, except James Welling)

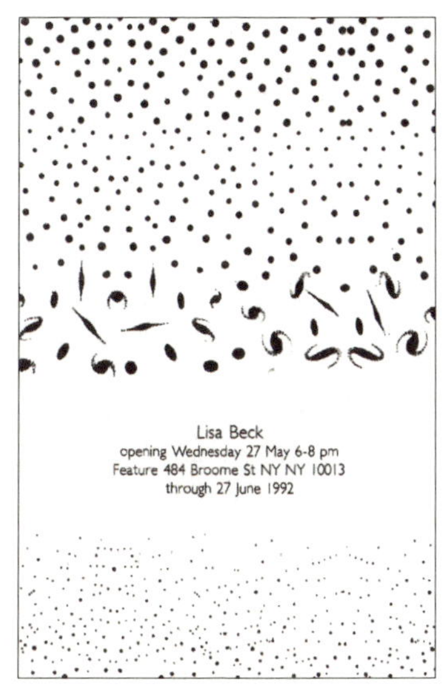



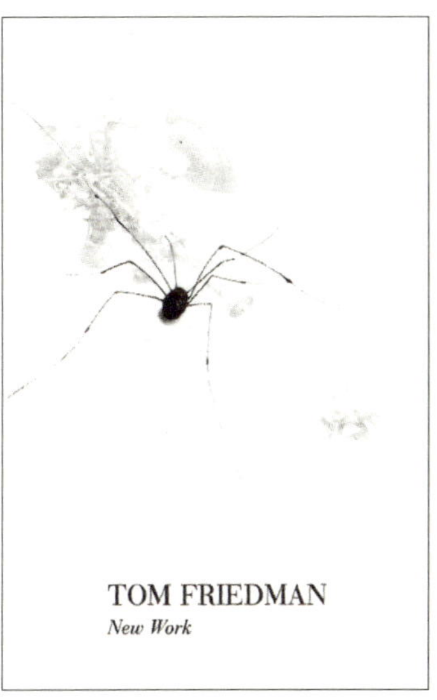



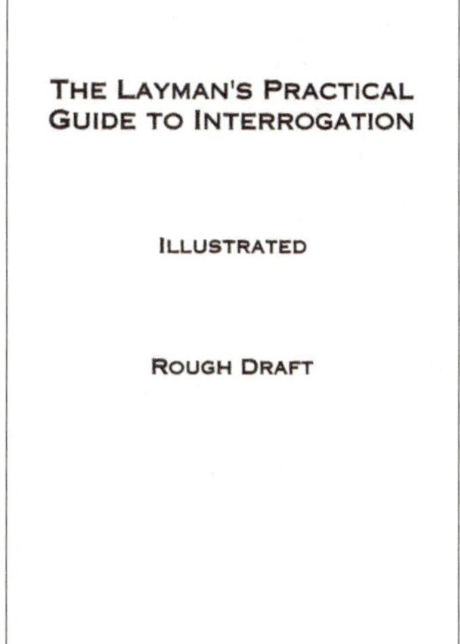



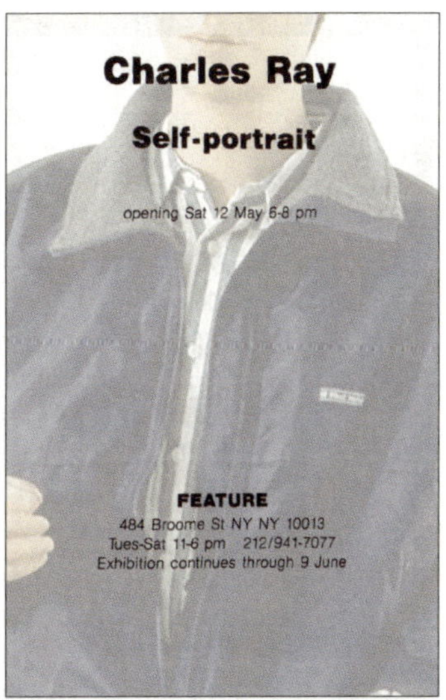



Clockwise: Lisa Beck, May 1992; Tom Friedman, October 1997; Charles Ray, May 1990; Hirsch Perlman, October 1992 (All New York City)

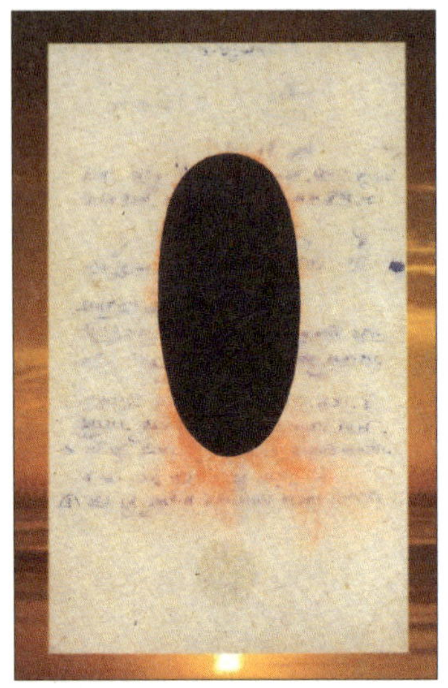

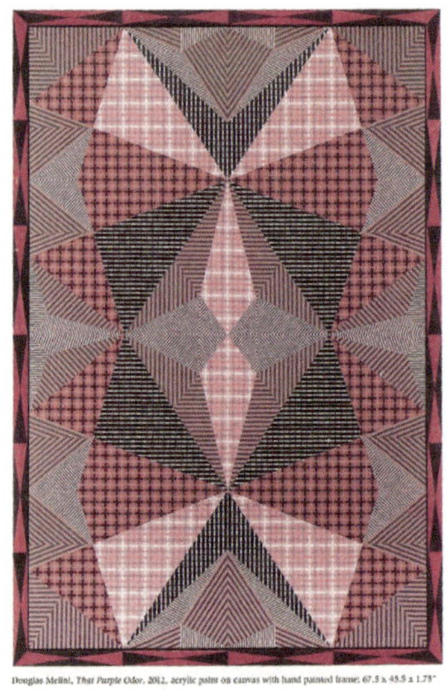

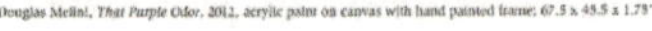

Douglas Melini, *That Purple Odor*, 2012, acrylic paint on canvas with hand painted frame; 67.5 x 45.5 x 1.75"

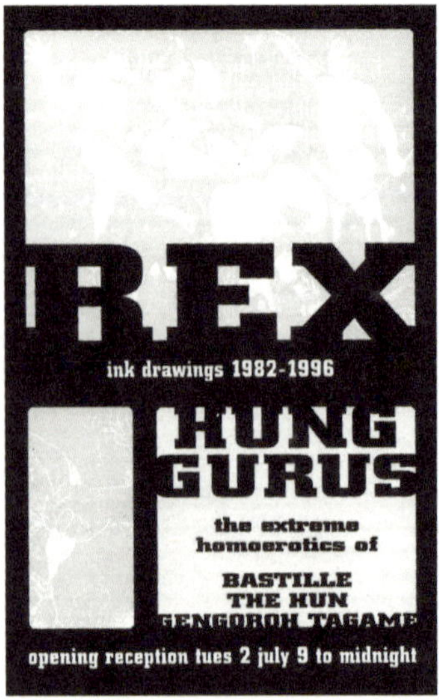


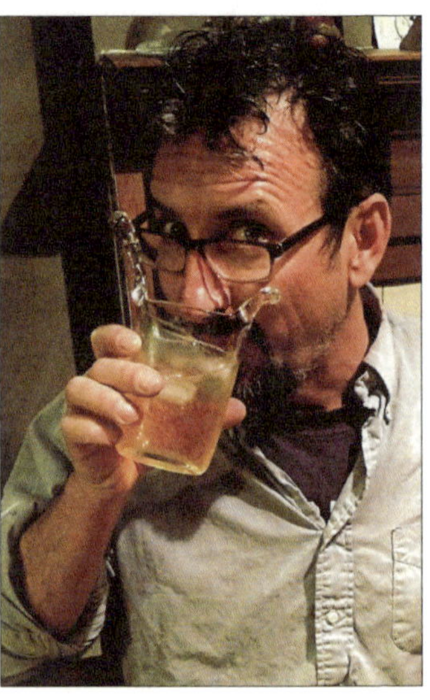

Clockwise: *Shiva Linga Paintings*, September 2007; Douglas Melini, July 2012; David Shaw, October 2013; Rex and *Hung Gurus*, July 1996 (All New York City)

as I recall. There were video nights that mixed work by artists like Jim Shaw, Ann Magnuson, Todd Haynes, and Carole Ann Klonarides with oddball music videos. Really great events. They were at night, so we were the only ones in this enormous building.

*How did you get involved with the gallery?*

I'd been working in design in Chicago for a few years and I seem to recall Hudson simply deciding that I would do the same for Feature. I can't remember even having a conversation about it. Suddenly I was doing it. I made the initial gallery announcement and after a few shows I began designing them all, and continued with few exceptions up until the final exhibition in 2014. Thirty years. Along the way I did Feature's various identities, and things like the *Artforum* ads, some catalogs, some issues of *Farm*, and a slew of other projects. An enormous poster for Tom Friedman. We worked fairly closely on these. Most of the time it was a mind-meld. When it came to the look of things, over the years we sort of became one brain. We'd throw out ideas, and then tamp them into shape together. In the beginning there were odd things like a fake grocery story circular that he made announcing a group show. And I recall an early Peter Huttinger exhibition where we decided the announcement would be a yellow balloon. It was really sweet. The information was printed directly on the balloon, so to see it clearly you had to blow it up. It came with a little cardboard stand of clown shoes.

There were also little secret projects. Like a later publication that we made anonymously—a thick, glossy faux catalog filled with art that Hudson simply wanted the world to see, mostly by people that he didn't represent. It was called *J'accuse*, although it didn't actually show a title. We snuck them into other galleries, free for the taking, onto counters or just in a stack inside the door. He also funded a zine that I made throughout the late '80s called *The Gentlewomen of California*. Again anonymous, and he would mail them out to a list of people he thought might appreciate it. A lot of these things were done through a not-quite-official entity he called Instituting Contemporary Idea.

As a friend and sometimes collaborator, it was complicated to also be a Feature employee. At one point at the 25th Street gallery, Hudson needed someone to work at the front counter temporarily and asked if I'd do it. It stretched into months, and in that time an outside observer would never guess that we were pals of some twenty years. I was treated succintly as an employee of Feature, and was expected to observe the strict protocols by which daily business was conducted. And it was a pretty rigid framework, especially as the greeter. But within that grid of exactitude, a disarming warmth was also to be projected. Holding two positions at once, like a zen exercise. [*laughs*] Also, this was intuited. Hudson rarely explained things like that to you.

*What was the run of the Chicago Feature?*

Just over four years. When the gallery relocated to New York I remained in Chicago, but we continued to work over the phone, via FedEx and so on. Later on through email. I was on call. There were often late night phone messages because Hudson would have a brainstorm for something he wanted made. Delightful, funny things. It was all part of this ongoing project of subtle subversion.

*Was Hudson a social person in Chicago?*

Yeah, he was out and about. Social and also sexual. I want to say "as many creative people are." [*laughs*] We spent time in gay bars and clubs all over the North Side, and in that era there was a lot to choose from. The Gold Coast is where he first saw the full-sized murals of Etienne, a Chicago artist whose work you could say is a counterpart to Tom of Finland's and Bastille's. Over the years it was interesting to see that what Hudson was seeking out sexually himself was as atypical and experimental as what he was looking for in art. They were two supercharged halves of himself, each feeding into the other like sybaritic twins. I also think that's why it was an obvious step to show explicit gay art alongside the other work in the gallery. He just thought of them both as equally startling and substantive, conceptually. And he began making paintings himself, under the name Johnny Pixchure.

*When was this?*

Hmm, probably 1984 or '85. Text and word things were always of real interest to Hudson. He would sometimes refer to himself as post-literate, but he was madly taken with language. He understood that even pornographic writing, like you found in either *Straight To Hell* or "vanilla" skin mags you could get at a newsstand, was something to pull apart, look at, and re-cast. That was the basis for the Johnny Pixchure word paintings. Of course during these years AIDS was killing people we knew, ACT-UP and Queer Nation were forming, and along with the safe sex mantra there was a contrary rise in expression around fetish and "aberrant desire." A byword of that era—"desire." So sex and queerness were of course going to be part of Feature's program, especially in those early years.

*Hudson showed Bastille's work a few years later. Much raunchier.*

The first Bastille show was pretty rough stuff. But he said someone wrote that it was more conceptually rigorous than Tom of Finland. [*laughs*] He felt like that was a small breakthrough, for it to be written about at all.

*There are stories of Hudson not showing deference to big collectors.*

As the art world, and dealers especially, became increasingly competitive and cutthroat, Hudson resisted as much as possible. It wasn't always successful and of course you have to play the game to some extent. But he never did more in that direction than he felt he had to.

There's a story that a very prominent collector appeared at Feature one day with a gaggle of assistants. This guy's speculative buying up and auctioning off had put dents in a number of artists' careers, and of course most galleries sucked up anyway. Hudson simply walked up to them and asked them to leave. Apparently they were quite perplexed.

*In what ways would you say his personality influenced Feature?*

Well, here's an example. Hudson was always interested in—and delighted with—the ways that art, music, film, etcetera affected cognizance on a neurological level. The '90s were the advent of designer drugs and the availability of synthetic DMT. I remember once having a conversation where he asked me to name the one significant difference between art and these particular drugs. Because the subjective experience of art was projected to you by others while the subjective experience of drugs was created by you alone. Later, a friend of his was able to procure DMT. It was reputedly lab-produced for research, so essentially different sessions could be conducted at matching doses. I'm not sure how many times he used it, but I know it had a lasting effect on his view of consciousness, which he was already looking at closely through the lens of things like Vedanta and meditation and diet. He mentioned his DMT experience to me numerous times over the years in terms of it having provided him an elevated understanding of death. He also said it provoked new ways of approaching art, uncovering less visible layers to explore. So yeah, of course all of that influenced what Feature was up to as well.

A funny story. Hudson took a road trip by himself from the East Coast to California in, I think he said, 1969. In Colorado he scored some LSD, and by the time he was heading up into the Rockies he couldn't drive. So he pulled over, climbed up a mountain and took timer photos of himself laughing and "watching the planet disintegrate," as he put it.

*How long had he been invested in the possibilities of hallucinogens?*

It sounded as if he had used them quite a bit in his earlier years. One adventure he talked about involved oversized caps of mescaline, and his friend Rene and him attempting to ride bikes from Manhattan to West Haven, Connecticut. After a few hours they eventually gave up. And I'm now remembering doing some psychedelic with him myself in Chicago, ostensibly to watch Michael Clark's *Because We Must*, a dance performance video Clark made with Charles Atlas. Hudson pointed out all of these oracular, unconscious correlations throughout. Having been a dancer himself, he felt that he grasped Clark's every intention. I was impressed. He was running the VHS tape back and forth and slow-mo-ing it so that we could get up and do certain movements along with it. I wish I had a video of *that*.

*Was Hudson in any sense religious or spiritual?*

He was interested in Vedanta, and particularly Ganesh with his trunk and many arms. But I couldn't tell you what the level of his belief might have been. It certainly wasn't doctrinaire. In fact, he once wrote me in an email, "Belief is an outmoded Aristotilean category." [*laughs*]

As far as spiritual practice went, he traveled every year to Fairfield, Iowa to the Transcendental Meditation compound there. He was most interested in the Ayurvedic workshops. Some of them sounded quite interesting. But if there was an organized *religious* side to why he went there, he didn't bring it up to me. I'm a dyed-in-the-wool atheist, and Hudson compartmentalized people to a degree, so perhaps even I didn't know that side of him. You could surely deduce an interest in Eastern spirituality, considering the five or six exhibitions of Tantra paintings that Feature did over the years. Also the *Legomandala* piece made on the gallery floor by Kylin. The healing machines by Family Research Systems that he showed would slot in there too.

But another way of looking at it, rather than putting it onto some vague sprirituality, it's easy to see the art that he showed as part of his own long, tapering scrutiny of reality. I say "tapering" because in later years he reached a vanishing point on a number of these investigations. His objective reactions were no longer examined with quite the same attention. He still ran the gallery like a zen drill sergeant, but it seemed like he became more cooperative with the world, more delighted than questioning.

He loved Jamestown, New York, where I later lived, and surrounding Chautauqua County. Rolling green hills and organic farms with produce stands everywhere. He would come to stay every summer. He said it was the only place he could spend an entire week relaxing. It was easier meditating away from the city. We watched a lot of movies, something we'd done in Chicago decades before. Going to the movies was our general date back then. And in Jamestown he'd spend hours preparing dhal. Tasting it, changing it, deciding which other dish to serve alongside, or what order of layering ingredients. We ate dhal all the time, and it was never made the same twice. He joked that if he didn't run the gallery, he'd like to have a little Lower East Side storefront instead that only served various takes on dhal. He was going to call it New York Dhals.

*In the later years Hudson did seem ready for something different.*

Yes, and change mostly didn't scare him. For example, during the Hurricane Sandy blackout in 2012, he vaporized. The gallery was closed and his phone went only to voicemail. There wasn't an announcement on the Feature website, and during the first week he contacted no one, even though he could simply walk some blocks north of his apartment to where cell activity resumed. I was living eight hours west in Jamestown, and although our usual four or five calls a week had suddenly stopped, I wasn't particularly worried. With anyone else I'd probably be anxious by the second day, but with Hudson that would be silly. Even inconsiderate. When he did surface a week later he told me he'd simply made an adjustment of perspective. His apartment had become a candle-lit ashram where he spent the days steaming vegetables on the gas stove, meditating, reading, and having talks with Kelly King, a friend who stayed stranded with him.

Later in an email, she told me how they spent the time:

> talking about what you do without signs. when things are hard. and
> you dont know if you are suppose to be quitting/remember it was a
> very long time without power/it was city camping/that we walked
> in pitch darkness and the city felt like it was time traveling back
> to a frontier town/we looked at giant beams on top of cars and H
> said 'See NY is still here'/like what is the big fuss/we passed jerry
> saltz in the dark

When he finally phoned me, he said he was having a terrific time and hoped that blackouts would happen more regularly. You know, he'd always been like this, but I feel like calling him fearless would only be acknowledging a flourish on something quite a bit broader. [*laughs*] If he hadn't disliked *Star Trek* so much, I'd be tempted to call it "Vulcan."


## RICHARD REZAC

*Artist and educator*

I met Hudson on the phone, long distance. Julia [Fish] and I were living in Portland, Oregon. She got a one-year visiting artist job at the University of Iowa in Iowa City. Also there with a similar position was an artist from Chicago, Richard Deutsch. They became fast friends, and on occasion Julia came into Chicago with him. At one point Richard said his partner Bruce Clearfield was going to have a show at this new gallery called Feature. Hudson was just opening, in 1984. Richard said Julia should go look at it because they were going to be showing interesting art. So she walked in and Hudson was licking stamps for announcements. They had a conversation and she liked him a lot. When she got back to Iowa City she faxed me that the work that was on the wall looked like it would be consistent with what I was doing, and I should send him slides.

When Hudson got them he called me up and asked could I send him three sculptures from the slide sheet. I said sure, I did, and when he got them he said he'd like to offer me a solo show. All of this transpired in the matter of two weeks. We had just spoken on the phone a couple of times.

*That's extraordinary.*

So I went to Iowa at Christmas, and the Chicago show I think was in February, a few months after he and I first spoke. I went in on a Greyhound bus, we met, and I hung the show. I didn't know quite what I was getting into, but it moved forward from there. The next year he wanted to have a show with Julia and I both, and we did that.

*You showed almost twenty-five times over thirty years at Feature.*

And maybe like other artists there it was curious in that I didn't get to know him on a personal level. He was always very clear and supportive of me, and he was always very comfortable. But there was a certain aspect to Hudson that didn't allow for a kind of social or personal conversation about his life. I didn't volunteer much about my personal life either, nor did he inquire. He wasn't disinterested, but he didn't pursue it. Hudson on the one hand was businesslike, for sure, but he was also warm—he had a certain look in his eyes that never made me uncomfortable. But my connection to him only went so far, and it really revolved around work and exhibitions.

*Did you find him sensitive to the work?*

Yes. With the interviews that he did [*Q&As with Feature artists, made into gallery handouts*], he did them consistently with virtually every artist. I don't know how many with me—five, six, seven. He would ask very pointed questions that gave me the indication he was wanting to know this other channel of information. Strangely, also, he never offered criticism, and I didn't invite it. He never told me I had to show one thing or another. It was always my decision. A degree of trust and acceptance that whatever I would put forth, that I would give him for a show, would have balance and a degree of completion, and variety, which was what I prized. He didn't reverberate back to me and say, "Now this is what I think it is, correct?" By his stature and manner, I think he understood it. Now, I'm one to leave the room when a dealer is talking to a collector about a show. So I never heard him talk to anyone else about it. But to be honest, I've never heard any other dealer do that either.

Based on the fact that he put his desk out front, he accepted all comers, anyone off the street. Whoever they were, he would engage in conversation. I have the feeling that he was democratic to the best extent when it came to running the business. He didn't judge people, whether they had money or not, whether they dressed well or not. I think he was just interested in conversation with people who made the effort to come see a show. Because of these certain elements of how he conducted himself, I always felt like I was in good hands.

I think now there are so many small shoestring galleries, run by artists and/or interested parties that are one-man shows. And that was true always with him. I mean, he had a great support staff, he trusted them, they did a lot of things with him, and they were loyal. But it was in his head, and his heart I suppose, that decisions were made. Not that he didn't invite opinion and input from others, but that was one of the distinguishing factors, that he was so much of a singular entity. He was also interested in exhibiting artists who worked in a relatively slow manner. Who were engaged by using their hands more than, in relative terms, others. There wasn't a lot of mechanical production or outsourcing in the work. The photography he showed tended to be… I guess I would characterize it as somewhat low-tech. The interest was not on the technical, but on something that functioned more like a drawing. Something that had modesty, where the subject was more grounded. The photographs weren't large or colorful. They tended to be small and black and white. And the occasions when he showed video, they were like that too. So I think painting,

.What do you think about the relationship of fantasy, abstraction and personal idealism in art making?
Well, those three words suggest an internal state or position, an avoidance or rejection, I suppose, of representation as we normally view it. And that does describe my involvement.

.How is your interest in a form or structure begun - from inside out or outside in; do you develop ideas pictorially or diagrammatically in a note book?
Diagrammatically, but I don't use a notebook. I rely on geometry as a language, but I use it intuitively. I begin what eventually becomes a sculpture by drawing in an exploratory way so I try to approach each work with little preconception. I think of the sculptural form as a whole entity, so I don't divide it, or think of it as originating from the inside or outside. I do recognize, though, that when a work is finished it can subdivide, or lose a sense of the whole, through color, reflective surface, repeated forms and so on.

.When you  work with a particular form for years, are you sometimes surprised to find where it leads?
Not exactly surprised. There is an unfolding that occurs and because my process is relatively slow and deliberate, I usually can feel what's around the corner. Baroque architecture is important to me and it offers a good example of a single motif, or principle, that can release multiple possibilities. In this show, spheres are in several works and the cap portion of the standing orange sculpture has been used in other past works - a tapered oval.

.Are there many preliminary drawings and or models for the sculptures and do these sometimes  unexpectedly inform the 2d/3d playfulness that seems underpinning your work?
Yes, there are always preliminary drawings, and I often make models beforehand. The drawings, of course, are not renderings but instead resemble architectural drawings and serve the same purpose - to clarify and set proportions - and with additional views, like plans and elevations, they can convey the three-dimensional relationships. So I can resort to a silhouette and read that sufficiently on paper to proceed. But there is a continuing exchange between two and three-dimensional perception here: a flat shape on paper becomes a volumetric profile which can sometimes look flat again. The models are made in an expedient material and full-size. I usually adjust these and sometimes radically so. I almost never determine the material or color until I have resolved the model and it's convincing to me.

.What has kept you so intent with the one to one human scale?
Well, it is the most obvious and constant measure that we have. It is much less clear or visible now, but certainly in past work I used a strict one to one ratio in determining the forms in my sculpture. Those that were a quotation of a part of the body, or the sources that were, or are, related to the body, like furniture, windows, architectural molding and so on. With sculpture that is abstract, I find also that this sensation - the familiarity of size - is a necessary pivot or mooring and so it allows me to incorporate more unlikely elements or choices in my work.

*2001 example of the Q&As that Hudson conducted with gallery artists*

drawing, sculpture were the areas he was involved with. That type of work is labor-intensive and rather unique, one piece to the next. There weren't many artists that worked in a systemic or serial fashion. They tended to make singular works, one after another. They certainly devoted effort to something well made, but there wasn't a fetish about craft or finish. It served a purpose only as a direct objective to make a work of art. And I think he knew what that was, he respected it, and that's where his interest laid.

The only other thing I can say [in that regard] is that there was a wide range of artists and aesthetics in the gallery. There wasn't a *look* in what he showed. People didn't go to Feature expecting one show after another to be relatively similar. The artists he showed did have focus and a personal take on whatever their interest or subject was and took time to dwell on that. There was an aspect of oddity too. That's why artists flocked to his gallery to see shows, because there was something about the pursuit and the investigation his artists made that was their own. It was personal. Not to discount artists everywhere else who make personal work. But there was something he could identify about some artists, and he let them loose. There was often in the shows that I saw at Feature a believable and odd quality. I didn't see that much then, and I don't really see it that much now. I think that did have to do with slow making and the hand-made.

Artists generally tend to gravitate to unconventional situations and anti authoritarian situations, if I can make that assumption. He was that. He wore t-shirts, not a suit and tie, and he seemed to not care what people thought of him as a dealer. He was transparent in the sense that he wanted to look you in the eye and talk to you. He wasn't someone who put themselves above you because they were better dressed or they had a fancy car out front. He himself was like the artists, allowing them to feel like they could talk to him. No matter what subject or at what emotional level, he was capable of inviting them.

The encompassing nature of his gallery was unusual, and in a way it was inviting for anybody and everybody. So hotshot dealers somehow thought they could barge in. I did see a few of those where some collector type— maybe it was a dealer—seemed to presume something, and Hudson wasn't interested. Even though it would have benefited him obviously. In a way he was a shield to the artists he represented by not showing them the ugly part of the art world. And he didn't bend over backwards to collectors, curators, critics. He didn't bow to them. He was the one who cared about what he was doing, and if others didn't and tried somehow to use him in negative ways, he could see through that.

What still probably most stands out for me was that because he was so respected by artists, they came to see his shows. When I encounter artists [now] who I've never met before, twenty years later they will remember "that one show at Feature."

## STEVE DILLER

*Friend and collector*

I think I probably was just out of grad school in Chicago, so I'm going to say it was probably 1985. And in *Gay Life* I read about an exhibit. The theme of the show was gay-related, but I don't remember anything beyond that. It just had a picture of Hudson and he looked interesting, and what they were describing also sounded interesting.

I had only recently started going to galleries at that point, probably about three months, as opposed to museums. Let me provide a little back story, because it's relevant. I'm a word guy. I'm not a visual guy, by nature. I didn't pay attention to painting, and I didn't pay attention to photography very much. I was very focused as a young man on politics and history and just trying to figure out how does the world really work. But by the time I got out of grad school, I was getting really interested in film. I wasn't focused on the visual aspects. I was interested in the way that you could create a reality that people chose to immerse themselves in for a few hours, and that was ideological. So I started taking film classes, and I realized after a few semesters that film is just as much visual as it is words and ideas. So I felt like I needed to grasp more about photography and about painting. I started reading about it and visiting the Art Institute, and was beginning to get an understanding of the design of visual spaces.

So I went to some of the local galleries in River North, which was then just coming up [as a gallery district], but I didn't like the way I was treated. There was an arrogance or smugness that they knew something that regular people didn't. That was really off-putting to me, partly politically because I was coming from this working class union kind of background and who did these people think they were? They're just fixated on their own creativity. And I didn't think I was any slouch when it came to intellectual creativity.

I'm walking into these art galleries, and I would simply ask the person working there, so, can you explain to me what you think the artist is trying to do here? And they could never explain it. I didn't give up, but I was getting annoyed. As a word person I sort of expected, well, if you're running a gallery, you can articulate what makes this piece of work distinctive, and you can discuss conceptual frameworks with me in the arts. Nobody would. They didn't want to, or they didn't think it was worth it.

Then I met Hudson, and it was a totally different thing right from the beginning. I still remember it. I walked into Feature and I told him, "I'm interested in understanding more about painting and about photography, and I read in *Gay Life* about what you're doing. Can you explain this to me?" And I got zero condescension. Just totally engaged, and totally fascinating to listen to. He blew my world open because I realized after talking with him for about fifteen minutes that there was so much going on within this work that was equivalent to what I was used to seeing in the political world. Yes, there were formal kinds of questions about the use of different materials and what fills a frame and all of that stuff. But then there was the deeper content about, what is this really for? What are we really exploring here? It had to do with history, and it had to do with the nature of the world. It was another way of looking at the nature of reality that I'd never understood before, because I was looking at that through facts of history or the behavior of large groups of people over time or class fights. This was more personal and it was deeper. It had some things in common with theological questions. It had to do with consciousness, and he could talk about that and he brought it to life for me so that I never saw the world the same way again. And it was never condescending, it was never arrogant. It was just kind of in the air with him. Yeah, he didn't start from the same place as everybody else.

I mean, I can sort of understand a gallerist who's thinking, well, how much does this person know? Because it's such a complicated story in a way. But Hudson would never let that stop him. The way that he thought was part of it, but there was something else there which was important, and it related to other things, other aspects of how he lived. Because he was incredibly empathetic. He sized me up within a few seconds and knew how to talk to me. That doesn't happen very often. [*laughs*]

Hudson had an understanding of people and human nature that was much more sophisticated than most, and I don't think he lived with it very well. Because it took up so much energy to live with what all of that was, with that kind of depth. I think it made him a great art critic and curator, but at the same time, I think it was difficult.

*At that time Feature was showing a number of the Pictures artists. You might say that they were trying to examine what art even is.*

Right, that first time I talked with him he helped me understand that every piece of art is about art. Nobody had said that to me before. In fact, everything that happened after I met Hudson was affected by what he showed me over the years. After I eventually decided that if I kept doing film I would be perpetually broke, my partner and I went to San Francisco. I didn't know what I was going to do there, but I fell into innovation consulting in Silicon Valley. I discovered that I knew, from things that Hudson had helped introduce me to, that I was really good at reinventing conceptual frameworks. And I got dramatically sharper because of it. So when I got to San Francisco, there were things waiting for me there that I could do that I never would have thought of. I could help Chrysler design the future of the electronic car. We put together twenty-year roadmaps for the development of self-driving EVs, based on the potential to deliver a range of experiences no one had ever contemplated for such vehicles. Based on that, Chrysler built a prototype presented at the Las Vegas Auto Show.

*It's impressive that you can discern such a clear arc from one to the other. What especially intrigued you once you began going regularly to Feature?*

Well, I remember seeing the Richard Prince stuff and asking him, why would somebody just rephotograph things? Or why would someone take picture of dioramas? I remember asking questions like that, and the simplest explanation just rolled off his tongue. It made total sense. And again, it changed my whole point of view about what somebody might be doing when they make art. I bought a Jeanne Dunning piece from him, the first piece of art I ever bought. It's about nature and how we label it. Yeah, that stuck with me. I've had it for a really long time. I remember going to see a show that he did with Jeff Koons, and saying to him, "But, what's the point of the basketball floating in the fish tank? Why is it $3,000?" Well, I later made a feature film partly based on what I knew about Jeff Koons. Feature just had huge impacts on me in all kinds of different ways.

*This was also a newer generation in the '80s. For you to have been their age must have been compelling.*

It was a generational thing, and now I look back on it and I understand better. Okay, well, here's how this was emerging and here's why it did, when it did, as much as you can say that. Here's who influenced it and why it seems like that had the impact that it did. At the time, it did align with other things that I was going through or that I was thinking about. It was the same time that we were in kind of high Reaganism, with everything that brought. In terms of consumerism and the way that HIV wasn't dealt with and everything else, it clicked into place and kind of helped provide me with a far more complete perspective on what people were capable of exploring, and through different means than what I was used to. I met all kinds of interesting people in the process as well, because Hudson opened doors for me to people I never would have met.

## LYNNE WARREN

*Curator*

Hudson lived in my neighborhood, so I remember seeing him around once in a while and trying to strike up a conversation, which even if he knew you was not the easiest thing. I always respected him and thought that he was serious-minded, and I had a cordial but not by any means overly intimate relationship with him.

But I absolutely remember the first Feature opening, because no one knew that he was doing it! [*laughs*] Suddenly he was like, I'm opening this place. I had the impression that it was somehow involved with *P-Form*, the performance journal. That he was going to go off and publish that, and have an office for it. So I wasn't even totally clear that it was a gallery. And suddenly we got the announcement for the opening.

I was bowled over because I think around that same time we had a director at the Museum of Contemporary Art who was very focused on kind of the New York thing. A lot of the people Hudson was showing, I had heard of or was already looking at—like Jeff Koons—for other purposes at the MCA. So it was sort of like, whoa, this is great, I can see this stuff here in Chicago that I've only heard about or I have to make a trip to see.

Plus he was showing some of the L.A. people. I really will never forget the first time I saw Charles Ray's work there, who I'd kind of heard about. He showed that amazing piece that had the printer's ink in it, the bathtub piece *Tub with Black Dye*.

My memory is that the collectors here… There were your Imagist collectors for sure, there still are, and they weren't interested. But the more forward-looking collectors, like Donna and Howard Stone and a few others, they just glommed on. Maybe part of it was Rhona Hoffman, through her support. My impression, and perhaps not in the initial year, but certainly very soon afterwards, was that he had some pretty supportive Chicago collectors going in there and buying. Many of them were going for the more emerging Chicago artists or maybe some of the emerging New York people, but he definitely had really good collector interest and, I think, collector support.

My viewpoint as a curator at the MCA at that time was that he was completely in line and in sync with a lot of what our interests were. Galleries had their purviews, and they certainly didn't feel threatened by something like what Hudson was doing. I've known these dealers for so many years, and they were always very supportive of each other—because they were always kind of beset by New York. And now more recently, L.A. So I think that people were also supportive of him. They maybe thought that he was a little quiet, and maybe he didn't want to become a member of the Chicago Artist Dealer Association necessarily. But I think they were very glad that he was showing this new generation, especially when he started including the Chicago people, who really ended up being very important to our city quite quickly, like Tony Tasset or Jeanne Dunning.

What I really appreciated about Hudson was that he wasn't the kind of dealer who expected you to come and talk him up. And he wasn't going to run out and talk you up, even if you were someone who could further his artists. He definitely knew who I was and my position at the MCA but it wasn't like he'd see me walk in the gallery and rush out to say hello or try to sell me on anything. But if you did have a question, or you did want him to walk around with you, he would be great.

Hudson donated fourteen pieces as a gift to the MCA. It came to us in 1997. He was always trading with artists for his own collection, and he had some really nice stuff. Included in that gift are some major pieces, like David Robbins' *Talent*, which now everyone wishes they had. We got it and we show it constantly. There's a Raymond Pettibon, who I think in '97 was just starting to capture people's attention. There's a Jim Isermann, there's a Robert Mapplethorpe. It's a really nice picture of two children. I was really touched when he did that.

I had this really interesting episode with Hudson. We ended up on NPR together talking about a show called *The Spiritual in Art*, which the Los Angeles County Museum did in 1986, and then traveled to the MCA. He mounted a show [in response] called *The Non-Spiritual in Art*, and we debated each other on NPR, I can't remember which program. It was controversial, and I think there were some letters to the editor of *New Art Examiner*. The original show was a massive survey, about how certain abstract artists were coming out of a spiritual place. It started with Munch and Kandinsky, and it went all the way through Duchamp and Bruce Nauman. It had Hilma af Klint and all these people. And Hudson was, like, "Spiritual?!" [*laughs*] It was like that was the wrong word to be using in relation to art, any kind of art, for Hudson and his cohort. That was quite a moment in Chicago's history.

## KEVIN WOLFF

*Artist and educator*

I joined Feature in '85, but I knew of Hudson well before that, when he had been the director of performance at Randolph Street Gallery. I was working on these red and black paintings of yoga poses that were a riff on sexuality. There was an opportunity to paint a mural at Randolph Street for some kind of city art thing. Hudson saw it there and liked it enough that he took me on. I was excited about joining Feature because of what I'd seen there.

*What struck you about it?*

It was a meeting place. It was the most interesting stuff that was going on. Let's see, I've got to say this as positively as I can. The Chicago scene was the same old tired, third-generation Imagist stuff. Lots of terrible painting, lots of terrible work. That's why I started doing the red and black paintings. I thought, "Well, I'm going to do these paintings, and I'm going to do them as dumb as I can. I want to make them as stupid as I can make them. But I don't want them to have any aspect of Chicago about them." That was my strategy. [*laughs*] It was really an antithetical move to what was going on there.

Hudson brought in so much fresh air. When you went to Feature it was like, "Thank god. Finally. Something to look at, something to think about. A direction to go in." That was very, very important to me. I was doing figurative work based on conceptual thinking. And that was something that Hudson appreciated very much, and why he included me in a lot of the early group shows. It was a good tension, and he was always playing tensions. It's what made all the work stand out. That's what a good hanging is to me. I learned that from Hudson.

On the other hand I also remember I had to fight him on things with showing my own work, that he was very reluctant to do. There was always a dialogue about how things should be seen.

Feature was what a gallery should be, but can't be anymore. The last discussion I had with him was exactly this. We were bemoaning the fact of art fairs. It's not a place that you talk about art, you talk about money. I always say to people, this is what killed him. You go into a real gallery and you start a relationship, a discussion. A conversation between the artist and the dealer, and the dealer and the collector. I've talked to a lot of collectors who've said, "I learned a lot from Hudson. He taught me how to see."

Hudson was not good at making money because I think he wasn't interested in it. And that's fine. But I felt the brunt of that a number of times. I would kill myself to do these shows, and then nothing would happen. If I have a complaint about Hudson, that's it. The only thing, really, but big.

I had a gallery in New York before Feature moved there. So I asked him, "How are we going to deal with this?" And he said, "It'll work out. Let's see what happens." I was dealing with the other gallery owners who were… [*laughs*] just awful people. They were always touting their gallery as "the largest space in New York." I had to meet collectors who treated me like the help. Hudson just called me up one day, after a year of dealing with this gallery, and said, "Okay, you gotta make a choice. It's either me or them." And I said, "Hudson, there is no choice. I don't want to be with them. They make my skin crawl every time I have to go meet them."

[Feature] was a place that was consistently interesting. It was the place that everybody knew to go. And the only reason it stayed open all those years was that it had a priority, which was the art. He was pretty much only interested in what was being said. I know that he let certain artists go who he thought were just repeating themselves. Hudson wanted to be continually challenged. He liked evolution. For years my work kept changing, and every time I would send new work his attitude was… "Huh." And that's what I was very proud of. I kept Hudson interested all those years.

*He was quoted as saying that he loved the way you "pushed the paint."*

Well, here's another complaint. He never told *me* that. I had to pull it out of him. He never told me what other people said, and he never told me what he thought specifically about my work. The last show I had with Hudson, he took my partner David aside and said, "You know, I just love Kevin's paintings. I always love the way he paints something." I said to David, "He said that? Gee, I wish he'd said it to me." I was both angry and touched.

# BILLY MILLER

*Artist, publisher, curator, and musician*

The woman who was the director of Randolph Street Gallery in Chicago, Nancy Forest Brown, introduced me to Hudson. He was her assistant at the time. To use a term that people use now, Hudson and I "dated" a couple times. We hung out, he came over to my place. And, you know, he and I had such different energies that overlapped in some ways and didn't in others. It turned out that we didn't hit it off that way, but we became friends.

Hudson became more involved with the programming at Randolph Street, and I came to everything they did. They had a really great show, for instance, with Alex Grey. I was impressed with the way Hudson saw things. So then, skipping ahead, I came up with some ideas for a couple of independent shows. One of them was at a building in the Loop that was being renovated, and they had empty spaces on some of the floors. Hudson knew this developer who was also an art collector, and he hooked me up with him. I did a show there called *Possible Worlds*. The title came from a Brian Eno record that I was into at the time. Hudson did this really interesting piece for it, a cut-out of a male figure, almost like a homicide chalk line, laying on the floor, with a tape playing of sounds of moaning.

I didn't ask him, but when we started drywalling he came and put in a couple of full days of work. Putting up drywall and painting and sanding. Oh my god, I couldn't believe that someone would do all this stuff. I said, "I have to give you some money." He just said, "That's okay." The next

We had planned another solo ses
sion with our popular ex-sailor
when the pool man arrived on the
set — and everything got serviced!

Johnny Pixchure (Hudson), *Painted Sextet*, 1985. Oil on canvas, 9 x 12 inches

year I did another show that Randolph Street oversaw. It was in another building being developed, and Hudson did as much work with that one as well.

About the time that I thought about moving to New York, Hudson opened his initial gallery in Chicago. He started showing artists that I'd never heard of. He had a Richard Prince drawing that I wanted. It was really cheap, just a few hundred dollars. I said to him, "I really want this, but I can't afford to buy it." He said, "That's okay, we'll just put it on an installment plan." I said, "Eh, probably not." I could kick myself for that now.

In those days what was popular was Julian Schnabel and big huge art. Sandro Chia-type stuff, which I was influenced by. So I did some drawings and he came over to my apartment and saw them. He gave me one of his famous critiques. "I don't understand why people are doing this. I don't think this is the future." Lo and behold he turned out to be right about everything. But at the time I was just like, "Huh! Thanks a lot." [*laughs*]

When he moved to New York and had the gallery on Broome Street, it was similar—new artists that I hadn't heard of before, that went on to be known. That was also when he began to focus on what he really wanted. I watched how that morphed. He always just seemed to go with what he had in his head. The thing that impressed me about him was this kind of contradictory thing where, on the one hand, his private life—what I know about it—was so all over the place and so weird and not together in a lot of ways. But when it came to his gallery and his vision, he was laser-beam focused. He would pull it together no matter what. I mean, sometimes I would see him and he would really look… wow, what's going on here? You need to get some sleep or something. But it didn't interrupt him at all. He would still do his business and selling stuff. That was the thing that always impressed a lot of people, I think. That he would actually *do* it. Art was the most important thing to him, it was his life. It was all or nothing.

He was also nurturing people. There were a lot of artists kind of circling around that he was interested in, but that he didn't think were ready. And then sometimes, eventually, they would be.

He and I had such vastly different ways of communicating. It got to this point where we weren't exactly feuding, but there was something where we couldn't seem to talk in person. And then email came along and we found a way. We became really close email buddies. Then when I'd see him in person, it was jarring almost. [*laughs*] He was always busy and I always seemed to catch him when he had a client. He would be so brusque with me, and I would just be… "What?" But then sometimes he would soften afterward. And that was the thing that was very endearing about him. He sent me a letter one time apologizing. You can't not like somebody when they're like that. From then on when something like that would happen I would just brush it aside. So then we developed this thing where we knew we liked each other. And he was always encouraging about my magazine, *Straight To Hell*. He really liked it.

There are a million other stories. One time when I was working at the Limelight, I had this idea that I was going to do an installation with stuffed animals. So I went around to a bunch of thrift stores. I ended up with huge garbage bags filled with giant stuffed animals. I was too cheap to take a cab so I dragged them on the bus. I took up, like, two rows of seats! And wouldn't you know it, Hudson gets on the bus. He sees me sitting with all of these stacks of stuffed animals, and he doesn't say anything about it! He was just, "Oh hi." I thought, "Is he not noticing this?" And then years later he said to me, "I always remember that time I was on the bus with you and all those stuffed animals."

One time we went to see James Brown in Chicago. Granted it's late in James Brown's career—it's not James Brown in 1965 or anything—but we were all getting into it. I look at Hudson and he's just sitting there. And he said something like, "Not into it." I was like, well, okay. Good for you. You're missing out on an historic moment that isn't going to happen in your life ever again. [*laughs*] But that's how he got to where he got. It would cause some people like me to bristle a little bit because of his abruptness, but I don't think that was his intention. It was just what he needed to do to get to where he wanted to be.

## DAVID SEDARIS

*Writer*

I'm just looking at a guide that I have to my diaries… and it was March 8, 1986 in Chicago that I first saw Hudson. He did a performance. And it just says, "Hudson performs 'Deep Kissing' and massages his ass." [*laughs*] I don't know that I'd ever seen any performance like that. I was going to the School of the Art Institute and people would do performances there. But that was all, like, rolling an orange across the stage really slowly. What people would tend to do was bring out a dozen props. And you'd look at them and think, "Oh no, do I have to sit through the blowtorch? And the Barbie doll? *And* the empty Jack Daniels bottle? What are they going to do with that?" But Hudson… I was always almost afraid of him. He seemed like someone with authority, like a teacher almost. Not that I thought he was going to be mean to me, but I felt the way I do when I'm around people who are a lot brighter than I am: I should just shut up and listen. There were teachers I felt the same way around. But I never saw their assholes. [*laughs*] And I don't know if it was Hudson who kept that distance there, or if I insisted on it.

I remember Feature when it was in that first little space [in Chicago], when Pam Golden worked at the front. I took my mom one time when she was visiting. Now, I would never have asked Hudson to look at anything that I was doing. But he asked me if he could look at some of my things. So I brought them to him. What I liked about it was that it was just like talking to someone who's kind of curious. "So, what is it you do?"

There was never any promise that it was going to lead to anything. And it *didn't* lead to anything. I think it's because that's the way it went. It wasn't me saying to him, "I think I've got something you're really going to want to see." I knew with other people, when they did that with him, he'd be like, "It sucks." He'd have people all the time trying to… At one point Chuck [*David's partner at the time*] said to Hudson, "I'd like to show you my stuff," and did. I don't know what Hudson wrote him back, but it was blistering. Chuck never let me see it. In my case it was him just being curious, so I showed him some stuff, and he said some nice things.

*You moved to New York not long after Feature did.*

I moved in September of 1990. That's when Feature was in SoHo. When I got there, Hudson already had an event set up for me, a reading at The Kitchen. He had also set up a reading at Simon Watson's gallery before I even moved to New York. That was with Richard Hawkins, in the summer of 1989.

*I remember that he was determined to have you seen and heard.*

He had already published me in his magazine, *Farm*. He let me put pictures in there too. It was a huge deal for me. It made a real difference in my life. Just to be brought in under his umbrella. Again, I never asked him for it and I never asked him to give me more space under that umbrella, you know? Especially if you're in a situation like he was, and in New York where everyone is so pushy. I mean, I remember going to openings at Feature and people would bring their slides. [*laughs*]

There was a limit to what he could give me. He couldn't publish my book or get me in *The New Yorker*, but he could sure get me started. He got me those readings at Simon Watson's gallery and at The Kitchen, which was a group thing. So I thought, maybe someone in the audience will say, "That was pretty good. Why don't you come and do this thing with me over here?" You know, maybe it would lead to something. So it made me feel like I wasn't moving to New York for nothing, or with nothing. I don't know if Hudson realized how big that was. I don't know that I would have had the courage to move to New York without that.

*Did you go to Feature often?*

Oh yeah. And at the openings I could see people that I knew from Chicago. Or I could drop by and I could see Jim [Pedersen]. Or Kay [Rosen] would be there when she'd have a show. Or B. Wurtz. I remember when I first moved there, somebody had a show opening. There were a bunch of people, and Hudson invited me to join them for dinner afterwards. But he didn't invite my roommate Rusty, who I was with. And so I kind of thought he didn't like Rusty. I should have said, "Oh, that's okay…" But I was so broke I thought, "Ooh, free dinner!" and I went.

Going to Feature was nice, because I didn't know anybody when I moved to New York. I did meet some people at Macy's. I met a couple of elves, but it wasn't more than that. Sometimes you don't need to be best friends with somebody, it's just enough if you can just kind of drop by and run your mouth for twenty minutes. It makes you feel connected.

*Both of the SoHo Features had memorable events, too.*

I remember an evening there. Hudson had this guy playing the guitar and singing. And the guy was young and really good-looking, and he spat a lot when he was singing. If you were in the front, you were soaked afterwards. I don't know anything about music, but I thought, "That guy is going to be huge." [*laughs*]

There was always an interesting combination of ease and discipline. What Hudson chose to be transparent about wasn't always what you would expect. For one, he had a very clear price list. Now, there's currently a show of Philip Guston up here in London, mainly drawings. So I went there, and I asked, "Can you give me a price list?" "Oh no. No. We don't have that." And I said, "But it's for sale, right?" "Yes." "You can't tell any-body how much it costs? Can you give me a ballpark figure? So I can be

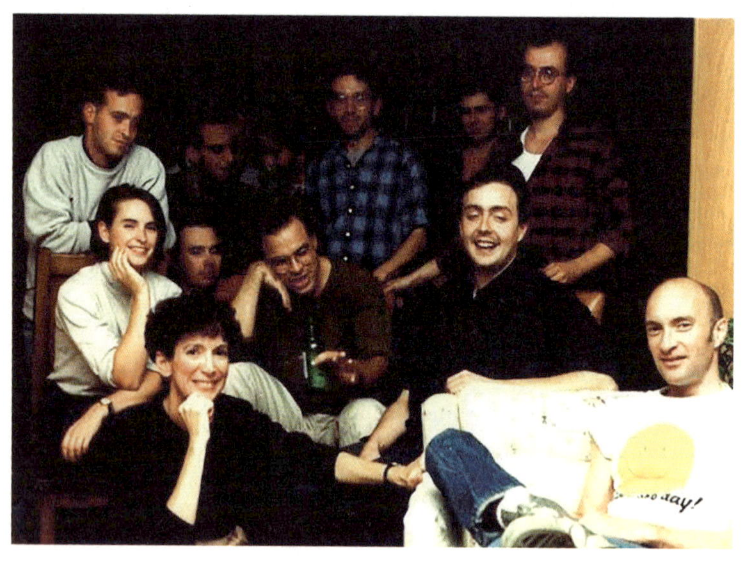

Farewell party at Kay Rosen's house, Indiana, 1988. Top row: David Sedaris, Chuck Gonzales, Kenny Corrigan, Rusty Kane, Steve Lafreniere, Gaylen Gerber, Kevin Wolff. Middle row: Jeanne Dunning, Mike Hill, Hirsch Perlman, Jim Pedersen. Bottom row: Kay Rosen, Hudson. Photo: Bud Rosen

thinking about it?" "No, I'm not authorized to do that. You'd have to make an appointment with our director, who could see you and talk you through it." I wanted to say, "You know what? I've got a better idea. Why don't you go fuck yourself." [*laughs*]

I just remember when Hudson opened Feature in New York there was this article, "Hudson Comes to New York," in the *Village Voice*. And he had a very definite look in the photo. And then you'd see him around, with these wild shirts on, riding his bike. He was great. And he'd always show you the price list.

## GREGORY LINN and CLAYTON PRESS

*Collectors and fine art advisors*

Clayton: At Feature in Chicago, Hudson was showing you something different. He was bringing in something entirely new and fresh. I think to me that was the real hallmark of what Hudson did. And he was an iconoclast. He was young, he was enthusiastic, and he was very welcoming and very warm. So it was really easy to kind of hang out with him and discuss ideas. Once we left Chicago the relationship changed. Frankly, I don't know if he had the same or different relationship with many other people. But I can tell you this, that there weren't then and aren't now a lot of collectors willing to take risks. We were both. Being young professionals we didn't have a lot of money, but actually had expendable income. So we were the perfect kind of clients to come in because of our interest. We were highly motivated, we had an appetite, and we were willing to make sacrifices in our lifestyle to buy art, as opposed to having to pay for private schools or universities or mortgages on a house.

Gregory: When we started with Nancy Lurie [Gallery], we were supportive and we were excited and we were collecting the artists with whom she was working. I think one of the things that was very important to Clay and me was that we would go into the gallery and sit with Nancy. At times we could spend two or three hours hanging out, talking about the artists that she was representing and that we were buying. We had really wonderful, meaningful conversations. The art world was quieter then, so you could sit with a gallery dealer and you could talk. Hudson's program was very different from Nancy Lurie's, but I felt like we had that same kind of relationship. Yes, we came when there was an opening and we bought some things. But we would also go in when we had no intention of buying anything else, because we probably didn't have the money—we'd already committed to something and we were taking several months to pay Hudson for something. But he was available and he enjoyed, as did we, sitting there and talking about the art that we had just purchased. That was as important for us as it was to actually own it.

There's one other thing that I want to get on the record. I think it's so unusual and it tells a lot about where things were in 1984 versus where we are now. Somehow he introduced us to Sherrie Levine's work. We were interested in getting watercolors from her. Clay was spending some time on a job in New York. Hudson said, "I will contact Sherrie and tell her that you're interested, and you should go to her apartment and see the work, rather than looking at slides." Clay contacted Sherrie and she invited him over. It was kind of one of these old-fashioned Lower East Side/Little Italy apartments, where there's a bathtub in the middle of the kitchen, and you put a board on top of it and that's your kitchen table. She showed Clay probably fifty of these watercolors that were based on a book that she was going through on Russian Constructivists. Clay was like, "I think we have some interest here, but I need to go back [to Chicago] and talk to Greg. But we'd definitely like to get some work." And Sherrie said, "Why don't you just take this box of fifty watercolors. You can take them back to Chicago for the weekend, figure out which ones you want to buy, and bring the ones you don't want back to me when you come back to New York." And that's what we did, and all the invoicing was through Hudson. It's indicative of a different art world from what we have right now.

Clayton: For me—and this may be a contrary view to what Greg has—between Chicago and New York in particular there was always a very strong interest in the hand-made object and conceptually-based work. It's kind of a relief, because thirty-seven years later reflecting on it, we did not get overly involved with too much abstraction. Hudson didn't show it. He was very true to idea-based work.

Now I'm going to jump forward to a very specific reason why we stopped working with him. He went through this period in the early '90s where he developed antagonistic relationships with particular artists. And because we're both friends with and collectors of work by two of them, we heard these things and our loyalty was first to them and not to the gallery. So I don't see him as Saint Hudson as many other people do. We paid far less attention to him after that—or I paid less attention than Greg. I feel like he had lost so much, both in terms of goodwill and good artists, at that time. He really needed to kind of re-establish himself.


## B. WURTZ

*Artist*


I went to CalArts for graduate school in '79 and '80. As students we had many interesting visitors there. One of the people who came, to curate an alumni show, was Helene Winer. She and Janelle Reiring had started Metro Pictures in New York, so she had not left Artists Space long before. She told me the new director who had taken her place was Valerie Smith. There wasn't a whole lot going on in L.A., as far as young gallerists and stuff, and I was curious about maybe coming to New York to see if something more would develop. Ann [Bobco] was into that too, because she at that point had gotten into graphic design. So we moved to New York in 1985.

It all kind of came together. We traded apartments with Kate Ericson and Mel Ziegler. Valerie included me in a group show at Artists Space. I actually had no idea then who Hudson was, but he was a good friend of Bill Olander, then a curator at the New Museum. Bill told Hudson about the show, and that he might be interested. He was often making these visits to New York from Chicago. He saw it and phoned me and asked if I would be interested in sending him slides. I so distinctly remember talking to him on the phone. He said he had this gallery, and I said, well, what artists do you show? He said, "I show Richard Prince…" And so I thought, well, that sounds legit. [*laughs*] I didn't even bother to ask him much more. I sent the slides, he put me in a group show in Chicago, and then a while later I had a solo show there.

*And you were with Feature ever after.*

When he moved to New York, people were crazy about that first Broome Street gallery. The openings were mobbed. The word quickly got out that this was a really interesting new gallery. And it was the most beautiful little space. Somebody described it as a jewel box. The little rooms, with the pillars. And they were right there at desks in the front, Jim Pedersen and Hudson, to greet everyone. I remember standing there and meeting Larry Clark, meeting Félix González-Torres, meeting whoever else. Artists that I knew of, but I'd never met them.

I had been showing at Bess Cutler, that was my first gallery in New York. It wasn't a marriage made in heaven. We had come to a parting of the ways. So when Hudson moved, it was perfect timing. The first show I had there, installing it with Hudson and Jim… Oh, what a delight it was. They got my work, and they had interesting ideas about how to install it! Of course, then came the never selling any of it.

As far as collectors coming in, I really didn't think in those terms. Which, in a way, is why I fit really well with Hudson. [*laughs*] Of course, later that became very problematic because I got in a very, very difficult situation getting older and never making any money. But that is not what I thought about early on. It was just very obvious that… wow, this guy is really into art. So I had day jobs, freelance jobs.

I think it was partly just the times. It's hard to sell sculpture, for one thing. And a lot of people just didn't get my work. After a show where nothing sold and I got no reviews, Hudson said, "Well, I hope someday people get it." And Dennis Cooper, who'd written about my work, said the same thing. Oh, Hudson *could* sell art. Some of his artists did really well. On the other hand sometimes people would come in Feature and he would be busy talking excitedly about some other artist's work in another gallery, about how good the work was. And I remember thinking, "Wouldn't it be nice if maybe he did that a little more for his own artists?" [*laughs*] But he had a kind of modesty that didn't always serve any of this well. I mean, he could absolutely talk about the work. He was brilliant in that way. Though I often think that a lot of the art he showed that sold well was part of the zeitgeist. It was what people wanted, which is often the way it is with any gallery. But looking back in my case, it just really wasn't the time for my work to sell.

One day I was in the final Feature gallery, on Allen Street. Hudson said that when he retired he would like to go work for Larry Gagosian. I laughed because I thought he was joking. But he said he was serious and I realized quickly that he was. He said that Larry had really good people working for him and presented amazing shows. I think in particular he was talking about those museum-quality historical-type exhibitions.

This was such an example of how Hudson never ceased to surprise me. He may have never tried to actually do it but in some ways it made so much sense. He could let other people deal with financial matters and he could just concentrate on the art. Of course, easier said than done for someone who micromanaged every aspect of Feature. [*laughs*] And micromanaging caused much stress for Hudson. But at the same time he loved it.


## LISA BECK

*Artist*

I had a show at White Columns in 1985. That was the moment when Tom Solomon was leaving and Bill Arning was taking over. And I had work in a show at Nature Morte, and American Fine Arts before that. I was very close to all the people in the Nature Morte family. But my work wasn't so much in the vein of what they were interested in, which was more conceptually based—Steven Parrino, Kevin Larmon, David Robbins. But it was because both Kevin and David knew Hudson from Chicago that they both suggested shortly after he got to New York that I show my work to him. That intrigued me because I thought, well, these are two quite different artists. He must be pretty interesting if he shows this broad a range of work.

I took my slides and brought them to Feature on Broome Street. Of course, you never ever saw anyone [at a gallery] projecting a slide. If you were very lucky they might hold them up to the ceiling light, but probably not! [*laughs*] So I went and I dropped them off with Hudson, who was sitting there and available. I mentioned Kevin Larmon and David Robbins. I didn't quite understand the etiquette of galleries. I didn't know that I was supposed to wait to hear something. So I never got one of the famous letters from Hudson because I went back two weeks later and said, "So. What do you think?" He said, "I like your work very much, but I think your titles are terrible."

I've blocked out most of them, but one I do remember was "Religious Experience." [*laughs*] I thought, well, okay, I don't really care about the titles. If he likes the work that's good enough for me. Pretty shortly after that he included me in a group show.

I think everybody's experience with Hudson is a little bit different. In my case, we didn't really sit around and go, "Well, I like the way you use color." Or, "This composition really speaks to me." We always talked about more philosophical things. Also, a lot of my relationship with him was kind of non-verbal. But—and this might sound strange—I'm really not sure exactly what Hudson liked about my work. Someone told me that he liked it because I took simple elements and made them universal and profound. Like I said, he never said it to me. But I felt supported, and I didn't feel like any expectation was on me to make something in a particular way. Or something salable, repeat something I had already done. Make something that would look better as a career move. That never was a factor in any way.

*Unusual.*

In the time I worked with him, Hudson always managed to have one or two artists that were very successful. They kind of floated the boat for the rest. For everyone else it was kind of "Just keep going. We'll figure it out." That was very special and helpful to me.

It was quite an ambitious program. He always had two or three exhibition rooms going, except in the last gallery on Allen Street. In terms of the way things were handled, it wasn't casual at all. It was taken very seriously. Otherwise, I think Hudson had a kind of an attitude of "Here it is. I sent you an announcement. Come or don't come."

One way I thought exhibitions were unique was in the combinations of artists he would do. And a lot of times the way he installed things was interesting. One example, I think it was a drawing show at Greene Street, there were forty or fifty pieces, but they were all hung in one corner of the room. The rest was empty. I don't recall the name. It was quite good, I've never forgotten it.

*You no doubt saw a lot of these aspects evolve in your time there.*

In the earlier years he showed work more often that had a sexual content. I wouldn't say that it stopped totally in the later years, because he still had Richard Kern and once in a while showed Tom of Finland. But in the earlier years there was more of it. I remember thinking "Hmm, let me check before I go there with my mother." But also it seemed to me that he started gravitating more towards—I sort of hate this term—formal work. Things that were more abstract and formally based.

To me, he was always still an artist the whole time that he was running Feature, which undoubtedly is why he did things differently. You do have other artists that become gallerists, but he *stayed* an artist. Actually, he was never really a gallerist. Do you know what I mean? He was just himself. He didn't change into another person to do that. And he didn't change into another person when he was talking to an artist versus when he was talking to a museum person, or talking to my father. And he very much trusted his artists. It was like, "I know you're going to do something good."

I recently saw that a young gallerist referred to Hudson's "radical inclusiveness." I would agree with that completely. His only interest seemed to be wonder.


## DAVID SHAW

*Artist*

I'd come late in my college career to even deciding to be an artist. I thought maybe I'd go get an MFA. But it was too late to apply for any of them, so I simply came to New York and enrolled unmatriculated at the School of Visual Arts, and started taking classes there. Within a year I was at Feature at least three times a week. And afterhours, because Hudson would work really late. It was the late '80s. I was rollerblading! [*laughs*] I would rollerblade up around Central Park and then come downtown and go to Feature, hang out and talk to Hudson, and then rollerblade home. I'd sit in a chair and watch him open mail from random artists soliciting his attention. He taught me much, and not even about the art world really—that was one of the least interesting things to him. But about being an artist and what was interesting. He confirmed things to me about what it was to be in that world and not get caught up in the hype of everything else. He was such an odd combination of showman *and* performance, but modest. He seemed to have so little interest in himself, but at the same time such a personality. An amazing confluence. We became fast, fast friends.

*Did you find him always accessible?*

Oh no. Of course the conundrum of Hudson was, "I'm in an office without a door. I'm available like anyone else is. I'm not special. You just need to ask." And I remember going there one time. "May I ask you something, Hudson?" And he said, "Next Wednesday I'll be able to talk to you." [*laughs*] By his own schedule he would decide that "I can't pay attention to that now."

*You joined the gallery at the beginning of the '90s.*

Yes. I'd been talking to him for probably a year, and he'd gone to my first group show in New York at an artist collective. He walked in and looked really hard at the work, and we talked about it the next week. But he'd never been to my studio. Then one day he called and asked if he could do a studio visit, and gave me a very specific time. The only thing you could say was yes, and rearrange your schedule. He walked around with his hands behind his back, turned on his heel a couple of times, looking. I had this twelve-and-half-foot steel stepladder, that only had steps at the top, called *Last Steps*. He looked at it, turned around, and asked, "Would you like to be in a show?" and then gave the date. "Yes." And that was it. "Okay, I'll send you the information," and he walked out. The first one he put me in was *Godhead*. And besides all of the other great aspects of that title, the announcement, made by dragging the image, pulling on it, making it stutter… that was genius. I met so many artists in that show.

*Some standouts in the twenty-plus years of exhibitions you saw there?*

On a very real level, every show was a standout show. Because you'd walk in and think, "What the fuck am I looking at?" Arnold Fern's giant heads. "Really? You show work like this?" Just so good. Or it would be Tom Friedman, who had his first show at Feature, and then many more. Raymond Pettibon. Charles Ray's *Boy*. And that's just talking about Broome Street. Once you get to Greene Street it's a whole other set of characters. Takashi Murakami's first show in New York. Nancy Shaver. And Nancy Shaver stayed with him. I say that because by then a number of his artists who had achieved a certain level of recognition had decided to move on, and left him. That taught me another thing about duplicity in the art world and careerism.

*I've been told that there was a point in the early '90s when Hudson sent his artists a letter detailing what he said were his obligations to them and also theirs to him.*

I've heard that as well, but I never received that letter because even though I was included in many group exhibitions, I wasn't represented by Feature until 1998. But I will say the beautiful thing about Hudson was that he was very clear as to what the terms of consignment were, what the artist-to-gallery split was, etcetera. This was all to do with exhibitions that were in his space.

*Some years later he sent another letter telling his artists that he would not be representing them in the traditional manner. They were now basically free agents, although would still be the focus of Feature's exhibitions. Do you know the reason for this?*

Originally Hudson mounted exhibitions with artists that he quote-unquote represented. But as certain artists became famous enough, desirable enough, to move out and beyond the gallery, I think they assumed that he would grow with them. It's my understanding that he simply made the personal decision that he didn't want to do that. That's not why he started the gallery. He didn't want to manage international careers. And he didn't want to expand his operation. He wanted to keep Feature at the size that it was and manage people's careers only in the States, and mostly in New York, where he was. He would even at times allow people to have shows elsewhere [outside of the country], and didn't want a cut of it. It depended. It was mysterious in that this wasn't true of all the artists. And there were people who were incensed by what they saw as this failure in his business sense. People got frustrated, especially those whose careers were blowing up. And they left, because they kind of had to. Half of them went on to have major careers and then half of them floundered because of that.

*You were with him for the rest of Feature's time. How did someone with such ethical restrictions maneuver running a gallery?*

He did nothing else. And would work regularly until eleven o'clock at night, by himself. Staff went home at six, he was there for five more hours. For years and years. He was doing all of the paperwork, and he was doing it by hand. He would, shockingly, keep hand-written records of everything. Even once computers arrived. He had a thrifty puritanical approach. [*laughs*] Though in regard to the artwork, he wasn't stingy at all. But at night he would wash the floor of the gallery by hand. Galleries hire people to do this, yet he just did it all himself. So his overhead was small but his personal investment was enormous.

Feature ran on a tight budget on one level. But he would still make sure that his artists got cards made, had ads in magazines for them, would take care of framing and shipping… all of the things you used to expect a gallery to do, to deserve the fifty percent off the price that they were taking.

*He was dealing hundreds of thousands of dollars worth of art on an otherwise very small budget.*

And not squandering that. You could almost say not profiting from it. Because Hudson didn't really take the money. He just put it back into the business. He admitted to me that he did it for himself, all of it, and his love of art. He certainly didn't do it for his reputation or for some, god forbid, social status. He just loved being around it. That's another reason he would stay so late. I would come down there at night to visit him and talk, and he'd be standing looking at the work on the wall. It's like, he's with it all day long every day, and three weeks into the show you come in and he's just standing there looking at it.

*The way Hudson organized Feature and his life were basically the same.*

Well, in some ways he lived an ascetic, monkish lifestyle. I remember he bought his apartment on 19th Street, and fourteen years later when I helped him renovate it he still hadn't unpacked the boxes. He was gallery-proud, but he didn't become house-proud until then.

*I recall his apartment as quite stark before that.*

It was stark. But as soon as he had to make a few aesthetic decisions in the renovation he just went completely... One instruction to me was that "I want the bed to go from one wall to the other wall so that you have to hop over it to get to the other side of the room."

*There was a desire there to challenge the way you even lived your daily life. Hudson told me a story of Alfred Jarry living in a space in which the ceilings were purposely so low so that he could never stand up straight. It would change one's perspective. Getting back to "an ascetic lifestyle," one of the advantages of that is it precludes anyone having much to gossip about you except that.*

He didn't enjoy nurturing the personal narrative. He loved stories, just not the ones ascribed to him. And even Hudson wasn't his full name. He had edited that down too. This was all to reduce the amount of historical narrative or personality-oriented information, and just assign a moniker to himself. But of course he was so eccentric to most that this attempt only built it up. They became *more* interested.

But a lot of people also ignored him. He didn't wield enough power and he didn't care. Because he didn't want to participate in the social scene that that level of power demanded. That was a life choice, really.

*It was a significant one. Most dealers are—partly—trying to attain a certain level of power, at least in part so that their artists get seen.*

Right. But he didn't go about it in any other way than simply showing the work. Again, that's why people left, because he wouldn't do some of the things that they thought going to the next level required. But he maintained—verbally to me—that that isn't what got you to the next level. Courting museums and courting collectors. He wouldn't sell to someone unless they wanted it. He wouldn't push something like, "You really *should* get this. This would be *good* for your collection." Unless someone had a specific collection and he might let them know, "This fits what you have. Would you be interested in it?" There was never a hard sell, that I knew of.

*More a heads-up. He once wrote out a list of reasons to place work, and a longer list of reasons not to. He wasn't a car salesman.*

Not even a little bit. To the chagrin of many, he only wanted to sell things to those who loved and wanted them. A lot of people think that the ultimate proof of the validity of a work is its sale, and after that its provenance. He didn't buy that.

*And yet he had a solid rolodex of collectors.*

Oh, collectors loved him. Until his stern, withholding side would come out. [*laughs*] But, for example, certain collectors learned quite a lot from him. They would talk to him about art, what it meant, and he would show them things and relate those to things they already owned. They so loved and respected him. However that's a complicated relationship, because they also supported him by making regular purchases. And that can get confusing. I myself learned so many ways of looking from Hudson. Much of the way that I look at art is because of what was shown—and how it was shown—at Feature.


## DENNIS COOPER

*Writer, critic, and filmmaker*

Feature was my savior. At some point in the mid-'80s I started writing for *Artforum*. I was doing reviews for them, like three every month. That's when I started getting involved in the New York art world, and had the mentorship of the notorious Christian Leigh and sort of that whole scene. I thought it was very interesting, but I could not relate to it. It was so extremely, you know, money and fame and all that. So Hudson was a total relief. Not only did he show nothing but great work—I mean, the gallery itself—but also his attitude toward art and the art world was... you know, instantly he was my great hero. And he's always been a big hero to me.

My memory tells me I knew him first as a performance artist. Not that I'd seen his performances. I mostly knew about him because of reading about them in *High Performance* and things. Then I heard from artist friends in L.A. that he was doing a gallery in Chicago. Everyone was very high on it. I met him when he came to something I did in New York. I guess it must have been a reading at Dance Theater Workshop. He was just there, and he came up afterward and said, "Hi, I really liked your stuff, we should know each other or something. Let's meet up."

When Feature got to New York, I hung out there all the time. I mean I went there *all* the time. For a while in the '90s I lived pretty near, so I just spent a lot of time at the gallery hanging out with Hudson, going to openings, and so on and so forth. I was never disappointed. I didn't always understand exactly why he liked something. But he had such an extremely pure and focused vision of what he wanted. So I spent time with the work and was always persuaded in some way or another to what he saw in it. First of all, he never showed anything that wasn't extremely rigorous and strange. But sometimes it would take me a while. I remember not really understanding why he liked Kay Rosen at first. Why do you like this? Or why do you like Lily van der Stokker? It just looks kind of silly to me, but then I'd sort of get it, and then I'd spend some time with it and I'd be, oh, actually this is hugely more interesting than I thought. And then he started showing Tom of Finland and all these other people like Raymond Pettibon. People who had not been shown in the art world before. He would contextualize these people in the art world, and that was really something.

Plus he was tremendously generous, and he was obviously supportive of my work. He let me do that "Farm Boys" theme for an issue of *Farm*. You know, he directed me to a lot of stuff, but he wasn't necessarily very open to the things I tried to get him to like. [*laughs*] He had his thing, and his thing was his thing.

*You were going to put together a show at Feature.*

Yes. At one point I was going to curate a show there. And it was going to be the only show he was going to let anybody else curate for him. But of course it did not happen because he did not like anything I wanted to do. So it started falling apart because literally he was like, "No, I won't show that. No, I won't show that." [*laughs*] I was, like, okay okay.

*You could see a little of that with his desk being visible when you were in the gallery, but his still seeming unapproachable.*

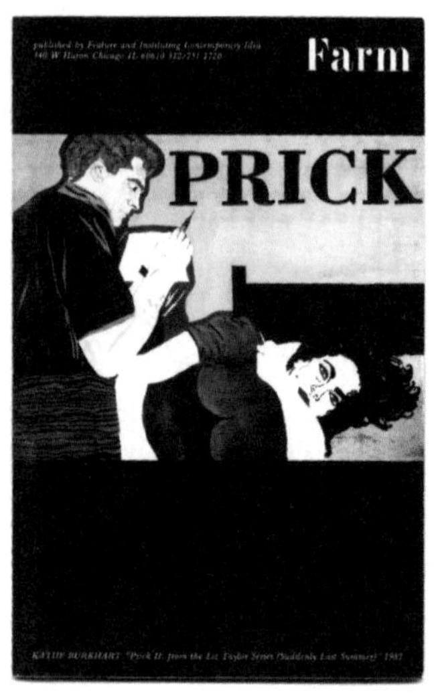


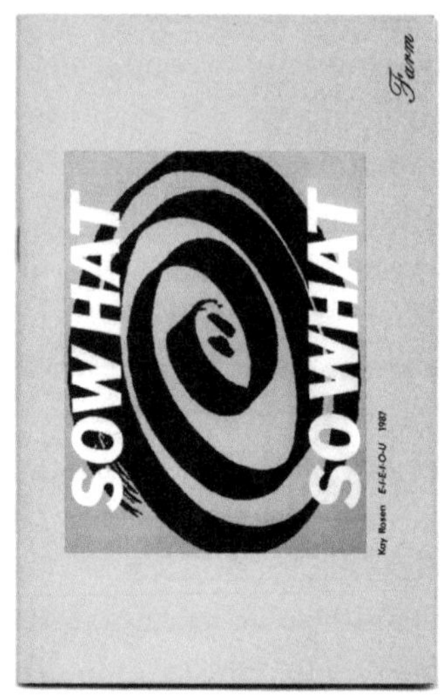


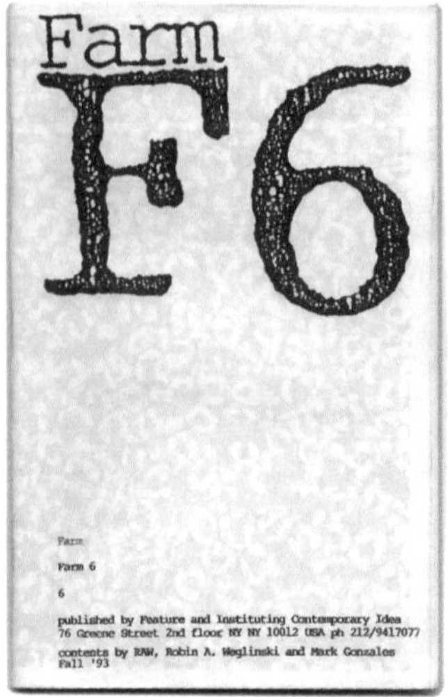


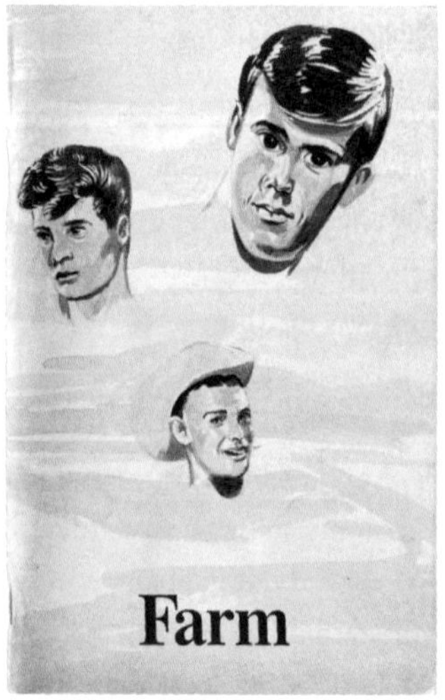


*Farm* zine, ca. 1987–1994

I liked that about him. I mean, I could always just talk to Jim. The thing that I think was really important, though, but it's very intangible now because he's dead, was that he was an enormously great role model. Other than the people who were actually there at the time, and experienced that and learned from that, it doesn't exist anymore. He was certainly a total role model to me. He was, like, "This is how the art world should be." I had been thrown into the New York art world, but I was not comfortable there. I grew up more with musicians and going to see experimental films and an L.A. art world that was Baldessari and Chris Burden and Mike Kelley, in a time when nobody gave a shit about those people. I was used to *that*. I was not used to this ass-kissing shit that was going on in the [New York] art world. So for me it was, "Oh my god, the art world is not horrible, because Hudson's there." I mean, to another degree Colin de Land was like that too, and Pat [Hearn]. But Hudson was the real deal.

*There was also a tenacity there to promoting people for decades who did not sell.*

Right. Like B. Wurtz, who I think is one of the great contemporary artists. He showed him for years and years and years, and I'm sure B. sold hardly anything.

*People use the word "helpful" about Hudson.*

Oh, he was extremely helpful always, but in his very strange way. He was prickly, and he wasn't the most emotive person in the world. And as you well know, he told you exactly what he thought. That's what I *really* appreciated about him.


## STEVE KNUTSON

*Archivist and music producer*

I had gotten the early Raymond Pettibon zines from a record store, starting in '78, '79, when they were first published, and I started collecting them. I found them really kind of shocking. In fact they kind of bothered me, but I was attracted to them. But the first piece of his I bought was a silkscreen print, when Feature was on Broome Street. I went in and I remember there was also a Mike Kelley show going on. The idea of seeing Pettibon's work in a public gallery was a real big deal to me. The idea that I could actually own one blew my mind. So I got my first one from Hudson in September of 1990, for all of $400.

*Did viewing it in public give you an idea of what Feature was up to?*

I didn't really have anything to compare it to. I certainly spent time in other galleries. In '82 I was living on Second Avenue and 3rd Street, above the Provenzano Lanza Funeral Home. I would go to Fun Gallery to see Keith Haring, Futura 2000. You know, go to Annina Nosei to see the Jean-Michel stuff. Go to Mary Boone and other places to check those things out. It was a really exciting time to get your toe wet. But later when Feature opened, I just found Hudson to be so much more. He was in his own world. I found his taste and sensibility unique and really attractive.

*Your collection of Pettibons is impressive. You went into the gallery regularly?*

Hudson would call me up on occasion and just say he'd gotten some stuff in. Always very forthcoming on things that he thought I might be interested in. Or he would send a note, or put me on a mailing list for Feature publications. But not just for me to spend money. It was more like, "I think you should know about this, Steve." Sometimes it would have nothing to do with the art that he was showing. Hudson liked to share things that interested him and that he felt others might like too. It was almost this education. Passing the baton.

He wasn't pushy, trying to make a sale. He'd sometimes be on the phone or whatever, but he was never in a big hurry, or would rush me. He would take me into the back room and pull things out, and say, "You can just go through this here." And he would leave me alone and go back to his desk.

I'd spend a lot of time in there and then I'd say, "Okay, I'm ready. How much?" He'd come back and give me a figure, and always take off some money. And then he'd say, "You know, I have to charge you tax unless you have an out-of-state address." And I was like, "Well, you know, my in-laws live in New Jersey." [*laughs*] There were even a couple of times that I didn't have a checkbook on me, and he'd say, "Just go take 'em." He was always totally chill with that.

*I know you also had a real connection through music.*

Hudson was really into music, and that's what my thing is. I don't want to compare myself, but I had a knowledge and an aesthetic direction in what I was interested in musically that I think appealed to him. So oftentimes we would talk about art, but then we would talk about different records or shows. He made me—I'm looking at them now—like, five different mix tapes of just things that he wanted to turn me onto. And I would make him tapes. Later on I would bring him CDs. Like, when all the tracking and outtakes of *Pet Sounds* came out, I made him copies and he loved that. He sent me this really nice note about how amazing it was to hear that record acapella and unadorned. How progressive he thought it was.

*You were a vice president at Tommy Boy Records in those days. Was he interested in, say, Stetsasonic or any of the new hip-hop?*

I don't remember ever giving him Tommy Boy stuff. It was basically electronic or psychedelic. Later on when I started Audika [Records] and I was [putting out Arthur Russell's unreleased music], I would bring him that. I introduced him to it, told him about his life. He loved Arthur's *Calling Out of Context* album so much. He even offered Feature if I wanted to do some sort of release party for it. He asked me to make postcards for the record, so he could send them out to everybody on the Feature list, and that's what he did.

*Oh, that's great.*

He said, "I want my people to know about what you're doing." I was blown away by that. I just looked up some of his emails and unfortunately I had only saved a couple. This one is from January 12th, 2004.

Hello Steve Knutson,

Thank you for the Arthur Russell disc. Just as interesting as the earlier. What a voice!

Haunted, melancholy yet not pressing/heavy, horny, great sense of observation, casual yet with an immense amount of intention and craft (honed beauty and specificity), humor and intelligence; very complex in a way I enjoy.

Seems I would have liked to have fucked with him and be friends—my ultimate compliment.

Thank you. It is so interesting to be moved by someone's creation.

So many right moves that any inadequacies or questions about style, timeliness, timelessness (greatness) etc. fall away.

A great model for how the power of the personal is outside of trends.

Again thank you.

*Going the other direction, what did he put on tapes for you?*

I'm looking at them now. One of my favorites is called "Hairy Forearm."

*Also the title of a Feature exhibition.*

Techno and electronic music were a big thing between us. And I remember him saying, "You never really pay attention to Radiohead." So he made me a tape of *OK Computer*. But on the *other* side he put Basic Channel, which is like, *fuck*, you know? He also made me a tape of *Siamese Temple Ball*, which was recorded in Thailand [by unknown artists]. Here's a tape of Oval. Also, he told me about Magnetic Fields early on, way before *69 Love Songs*.

*Just curious, were you social outside of the gallery?*

Not really. He invited me out to a dinner once with him and a couple of other people, and Raymond Pettibon. And I didn't go. I wasn't interested in meeting Raymond. I was too self-conscious. I love his artwork, it's just that I didn't want to meet this person. [*laughs*] And I think Hudson was a little kind of like, oh, well, you should come, but *okaaay*.

I did go to his apartment once and hung out. I think maybe it was because we were going to walk over to see Tortoise at Irving Plaza. I was really shocked by how austere his living quarters were. He had just a very small, basic apartment. I mean, it seemed comfortable. It was spotless. There was some art hanging up. A General Idea *AIDS* tapestry. Hudson didn't seem like the kind of person that really wanted to flaunt any type of wealth or financial success. It was just, "I have work to do. There are things that I love and I want to promote, and I want to support these people." It didn't seem like it was something that was tied into any ego or success, like maybe other people would've had or wanted to flaunt. It didn't seem like any of those things interested him.

I do remember that in the tiny kitchen he just had tons and tons of vitamins. He said that he basically lived on vitamins. But we would also talk about cooking Indian food. He seemed to be really into it. I think we bonded over that.

Hudson was interested in the trips that my wife Ann and I would do. We went to Tibet a couple of times, and spent time in the Indian Himalayas, and of course Nepal. I would bring back art. I bought some thangkas in Lhasa. I remember showing one to Hudson, because I needed to get it framed—he framed all my stuff—and he flipped. "These are amazing!" He was always blown away about the things that I'd bring back, and would make suggestions as to how he thought they should be framed. Sometimes we'd talk about Hinduism or Buddhism in relationship to the artwork or the travels that I was doing. I do think those interests were more kind of intellectual for him. It wasn't about the rituals or where you're going to end up if you follow certain paths. It was more the idea that there are these paths, these are what these people think, it's interesting, and could be applicable to my life intellectually. And then, you know, with the food and stuff, it's about health too. Was it something we talked about in any kind of detail? Yes and no, but how I viewed his interest is not dissimilar from mine.

In January of 2014, I told him we were moving to Portland.

> Wow Steve K wouldn't have expected that. Congrats shang a dang dang yes. We'll help more tomorrow. Is everything framed? Does your insurance company require appraisals or may they simply be valuations?

He asked me to call him about those things, and then when I did call him it was like one of the only times I ever talked to him when he was really grumpy. It was just sort of like, you gotta do this, do that. Don't do that. No, no, no, no. Listen to me. [*laughs*] But I think that may have been the last time I talked to him.

Hudson was a lovely guy. I really loved him. I was always kind of intimidated by him because he was so fucking smart and he had no time, no room for any kind of pretense or bullshit, you know? I admired him for that, but I was also like, oh man, I hope I'm not one of those people. [*laughs*]

## JIMI DAMS

*Artist, gallerist, and curator*

In the '80s, Europe was very much still in the '70s conceptual mode. In Belgium, we were coming down from it a little bit, but it was still hardcore institutional. If you did anything else as an artist you had no place there whatsoever. Which is why I moved to Paris. I wanted to see something else and to get another outlet for my work. That's where I saw the East Village art scene. I saw Rhonda Zwillinger and Arch Connelly for the first time in Paris. Then when I came to New York in 1992, a friend of mine in Belgium said, "You have to go and see Feature. It's going to click on every level." I walked in and I looked and I really was dumbstruck. I'd never seen art like what was on display there anywhere before. I went back a few times. Didn't speak to Hudson, I just looked. When I returned home, I kept thinking about it and kept thinking about it. Email was almost non-existent, and I was a fervent letter writer. I hated phone calls. So I wrote Hudson a letter saying how impressed I was and how much I appreciated what was going on there. It was a breath of fresh air. It really encouraged me to continue doing what I was doing. Hudson immediately wrote back and thanked me for that and talked a little bit. And then basically we wrote each other every week after that. We kept writing, writing, writing. He sent me the G.B. Jones book, and talked about that. Well, he just sent me tons of stuff. I sent him tapes and books. And then on my next visit a year later, we met and became friends.

By 1997 we were very close. I came to New York because I had a show at Gracie Mansion. But I had told him I would not see him, because I was in a very bad place, and I thought it was bad enough to have to deal with it myself. He knew that I had attempted suicide and knew I was depressed. He said, "I don't care, I want to see you anyway. You don't need to make any effort, I just want to see you." So I decided I would meet him for a short while at Angelika. After that I went to Gracie's, did the show, and came back to Europe. By the time I was home there was a fax on the floor from Hudson, saying "You need to come to the United States right now. I want you to come work at Feature. You need a change of environment. Think about it and let me know." I was a teacher, full time. I had tenure. I was set for life. My shrink said, "You need to do it." So I did. And it made a ton of difference. I always said to him, until a couple of weeks before he died, "You literally saved me. You gave me another shot at life."

Sometime the next year I was walking with him, and he said, "I had a dream about you. We were walking on 2nd Avenue. You were a little child and I was holding your hand. I put my hand on your head. I felt the need to protect you." I said, "Well, that's funny because that is exactly the feeling I get from you. That is what you do." I never had a father figure. We were a bit far away age-wise, but I considered him exactly that. After my first stint at Feature, in 1998, I was still here on a tourist visa. I wasn't officially working there. He said, "What do you think, do you want to stay? I think you should." How was I going to do that? He said, "We'll just apply for a visa." And that is how I stayed.

*Did you feel at the time that Feature had a discernible vision?*

My interpretation of it was that… this was him. Everything was him. Being an artist himself, basically what he was showing were extensions of what he was interested in as an artist, and found in other artists. In addition to, or a reflection on. That's why Feature was Hudson and Hudson was Feature. Without Hudson there was no Feature. It's why he always said he never wanted the gallery to continue if he died. Also, he knew exactly what to do if he wanted to make tons of money. But he had no interest in doing those things. He wanted to be comfortable, he wanted his artists to have some money, but that was all subject to the greater idea. That's why the last few years he was extremely discouraged. That was his life. It was him. And then all of a sudden these things that you worked for all of these years, these wonderful things you did, in this day and age it didn't matter anymore. It was as if everyone just passed you by. In the end, when collectors started dropping off, it hit him hard. You feel like no one is interested anymore. That was basically his thought at the end. I agreed. Because the only thing anyone was interested in was money. That's it. That was now the purpose of life: money. The quality of a show is only if it sells out. If it doesn't sell out, it's good for nothing. All of this went completely against his way of thinking.

*There were times when the gallery was flush.*

Oh yes. We were on Greene Street, and toward the end, before we moved to Chelsea in September of 1999, Feature began to make money. Hudson had to sell a lot of art in order to be able to even do the move. And then, when we were actually there, for some weird reason Feature became financially successful. [*laughs*] The most successful Hudson had ever been. But that changed back when he moved from Chelsea to the Bowery in 2008. It had nothing to do with the change of location, it had to do with the fact that everything collapsed in November [in response to the financial crisis].

Then there was this whole slew of artists he was really interested in, but that he would only show once in a while, depending if what they were currently doing was something that interested him. Sometimes there would be three to four years in between shows for these artists.

I think we were still on Greene Street, and a Feature artist began sending Hudson images of his new paintings. Hudson didn't like them, and he kept not liking them. So all of a sudden, someone who had been a stalwart for the gallery, a constant, someone Hudson had liked a lot, was gone. To Hudson, the idea and what was being done were more important than anything else. In my view, let the artist do what they want to do, and they'll grow out of it or they won't, and you'll evolve with them. But with Hudson, he made *that* decision. This happened a few times. Or... slowly, very slowly, an artist wouldn't get any more shows.

*Can you explain the way in which Hudson would represent an artist during your time at Feature?*

Hudson had binders for certain artists. But he also had "Others." Or "Miscellaneous." Or "Interesting." He would give these people shows, but they didn't have their own binder. If you moved to your own individual binder you were being represented by him. Although even that was different than other galleries. After he had worked with international galleries, and had nothing but heartache with it, he'd decided that he did not want to be any artist's primary dealer. Meaning if an artist would be able to get a show in Paris, he would say, "Yes, go and do it." But he didn't want to have anything to do with it. He would not arrange the shipping, he would not arrange consignment forms. "That is none of my business. You can do that." This happened often. Because, you know, you do with your gallery what you want. But when Tom Friedman had a show internationally, that was different. All of that had to go through Hudson. In other words there was a distinction with the moneymakers and the other ones. The moneymakers, he would want to control all of it. That way he could make sure that he wasn't losing the artist, and that he could give them his all. That created a whole brouhaha with [a Feature artist]. Not in the beginning, but the more it evolved, he started complaining that he had to do everything through Hudson.

When it was in New York and someone wanted to do something—for example, when a different Feature artist had his show at another New York gallery, Hudson of course was going to be involved, because it was in New York. The story is funny. The dealer sent a fax with the agreement. The consignment form, how it would work, the percentage division, etcetera. I gave the fax to him and he went *Pfft*. He took a really fat marker, drew a big skull and crossbones over the entire fax, and inside the head he wrote "NO." And he said, "Jimi, fax that back, please." After it faxed he said, "Let's count and see if we can make it to four." One… two… RING, the phone. [*laughs*] He picks it up, "Hello? Oh hello ___. Yes. Yes, I was shocked too." And very calm. I thought that was brilliant. That was also part of Hudson. He was, like, no, you don't set the rules here. This is an artist that I represent, the rules will come from me. Instead of going into an entire discussion, he stopped it right there.

*How was working at Feature different than other galleries?*

Compared to other galleries that I'm familiar with, Feature was completely different in every way. Each gallerist has their own peculiarities, but there are a set of rules that everyone basically abides and functions by. One thing that was different at Feature was, in the first place, no talking. You did not talk. It had to be quiet. There would be time when there was talking and laughing, but that was up to him. You wouldn't start yapping or asking something because he would shut you down. Because he was working, he needed to concentrate. And this wasn't just for the staff. When people would come in [to speak to him] he would say, "This is not a good time." And they'd have to leave. No other dealer would do that, that I know of.

Also there is not a gallery in the world that shipped things the way Feature did. Everyone talked about that. It was referred to as "Hudson packing." Before I worked at Feature, I curated a show at Cokkie Snoei in Rotterdam, with artists from Feature. A box arrived. It was the B. Wurtz trash bag trees. Basically they were just small, loose elements. But it was a ginormous box. Cokkie said, "What is this? It's such a big sculpture?" We opened it up and it was a wall of blue styrofoam. And then separately packed there was each bloody plastic bag! Every single thing was wrapped. It was really unbelievable. Cokkie took pictures. "I've never seen anything like this. It's insane." [*laughs*] Of course some people complained about it, because something that you could otherwise just fit in a plastic bag arrived instead in an enormous box. It was expensive. But you had to respect the artwork at all times. It was like, we're running a decent business here, it's not some carpet shop. He was notorious for it. On the other hand… Lucky DeBellevue was having a show in Paris. I happened to be going to Paris too, and Hudson said, "Would you mind taking the Lucky DeBellevue pieces with you?" I said, no, I wouldn't mind. I mean, I'll have to check in this big box separately and then wait to pick it up after I land, and then say that it's mine in customs. La-da-da, okay. So I go to pick up the piece. I go into his office and he says, "Oh, it's right there."

I look around and I don't see any box. "You see?" he says, and points to the sofa against the wall. And sure enough there it was, rolled in a ball. Because they were Lucky's chenille stents. You could stretch them out again, right? He's basically fumbled the whole thing together in a ball. It made it very easy for me, because I could just put it in a plastic bag and take it with me. I didn't even need a box.


## G.B. JONES

*Artist, musician, filmmaker, and zinemaker*

It all happened in a very strange way. From what I can remember, sometime in the early '90s Dennis Cooper got in touch with me and said, this gallery owner in New York wants to see your work. I thought, "Yeah, right." I didn't believe him. But then I told Johnny Noxzema [*friend and zine collaborator*] and he got really excited, as he alway does. He said, "Okay, we'll take a trip. We'll all go down [from Toronto] to New York. We'll visit the gallery and take your work down and see what he says." So me, Johnny, and a couple of friends drove down to Feature and met Hudson. Dennis had maybe given him a copy of *J.D.s* [*the foundational queer zine produced by Jones and Bruce LaBruce*] or told him about it, but that's where he knew of me.

*I like the idea that he first saw your work in a zine.*

It's amazing. He saw a xeroxed fanzine—not a magazine, but a fanzine. Amateur, unprofessional, fanboys, fangirls, fan art—it had negative connotations for a lot of people. That too was really exciting, that he would say, "You know what, those arbitrary descriptions don't mean anything to me. I'm looking for something exciting." I had not experienced that, especially in terms of galleries and the real quote-unquote art world. At least in Toronto. I had no experience with the art world in New York. I had no idea of what to expect. The fact that he was so nice and so enthusiastic was incredible.

*You showed him your* Tom Girl *drawings. He must have loved their reverse-gender take on Tom of Finland, who he also showed.*

Yes, and I'm trying to think of how many I even had at that point. Not many. You see, I only did them for *J.D.s*, and there had only been eight issues. I probably had at the most twenty drawings. That was it, my entire fine art career. [*laughs*] I was more concentrated on photography at that point, and film. The drawings were just a sideline. But when I showed them to him he, immediately said, "Yeah, these are good. I think I can use them." Again, my reaction as per usual was, oh, he's just being polite. I'll never hear from him again. So I went home. But the next thing, he's contacting me and saying, "You better do some more drawings, because you're going to have a show here with Tom of Finland." I was a bit stunned. So I had to spend the next few months drawing constantly.

*The summer of 1991. I remember how groundbreaking that show was.*

I'm glad we're talking about this stuff, especially for the kids. Because I don't know if they can even fathom. How can I explain it? The world has changed so much. When Bruce and I started *J.D.s*, and then Caroline Azar and I started Fifth Column [*early queer-core Toronto band*], in a certain sense we thought we've got nothing to lose. We can do what we want, say what we want, and live the way we want. We don't have any money or a record deal. But it wasn't typical or common then to be openly queer and be musicians, filmmakers, even zinemakers. If you were a serious filmmaker or a musician you stayed in the closet. And then you walk into Feature and you're confronted with, you know, my drawings and Tom of Finland. A very confrontational queer show. That was not happening in the art world at that time.

*People were startled that Hudson showed Tom of Finland with no irony.*

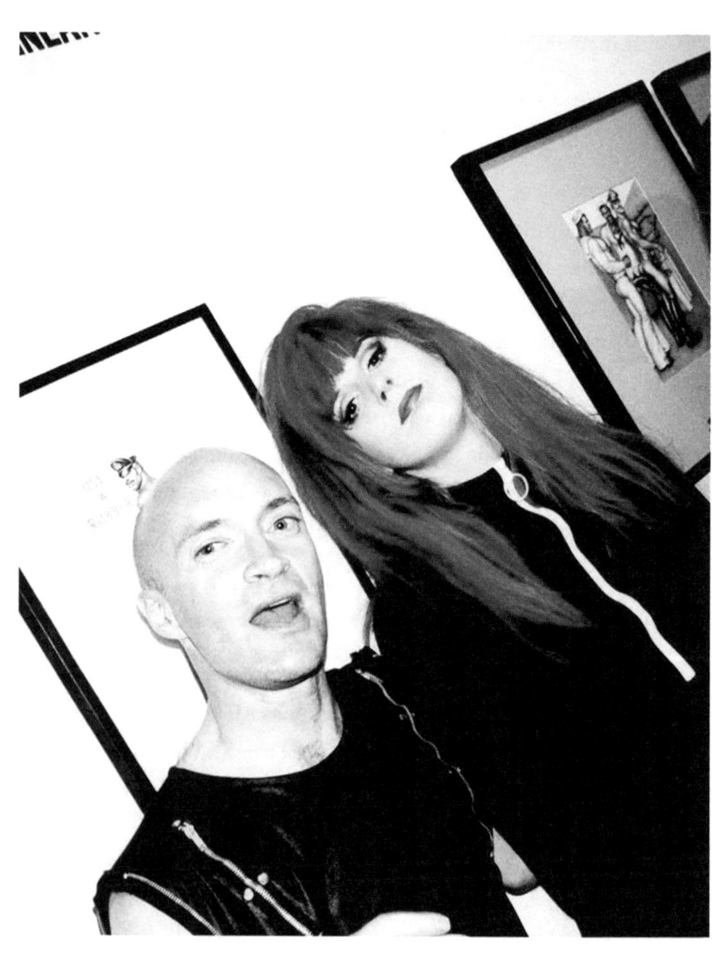

With G.B. Jones at Feature, Greene Street, New York City, 1991. Photo: John Richard Allen

And I think that's important. It wasn't presented in an ironic context. It wasn't put up for people to snicker and laugh. It was too shocking to most people for it to even be ironic. I remember going to the opening. Of course I'd been looking at Tom of Finland's art for years, so the impact had dulled somewhat for me. But I was looking around and I could see that even though this was New York, people were shocked to see it up on the wall. Hudson was very much a part of the queer wave, the big change. The zines, the bands, and his gallery represented a huge shift, from the end of the '70s to the beginning of the '90s.

*What was your relationship with him?*

We mostly talked on the phone, but he came up [to Toronto] a number of times. I remember going out to dinner with him and Robert Flack. Of course those years were kind of a whirlwind, there was so much going on. It was incredible how all these people from film, music, literature all got to know each other, many through Feature. I went to New York once with Fifth Column, and Rosa von Praunheim was visiting Hudson. He got Rosa and his boyfriend to come see us at CBGB. It was fascinating how queer people were interconnecting, really exciting. It was the first wave of a change that would become solidified in the new century.

*Hudson published the book* G.B. Jones *in 1995. It was under the imprint of his own zine* Farm.

Yes! And it's worth a lot of money right now. [*laughs*] I wish I had a stack of them stashed away somewhere. That was fantastic, and then of course it was banned in Canada.

*Was it really? You know, that certainly wouldn't have happened to many art books before then, simply because a great deal of contemporary work was not even figurative.*

And representational work meant something different when it was partnered with queer politics or aesthetics. Obviously you can say one thing about the work of art in the gallery, and its purpose within capitalism, and the heterosexual patriarchy. But once you started introducing queer subject matter and representation into a gallery in the 1990s, it's quite a different thing. It means something different than it has ever before. I think people need to give him credit for having a significant impact on the culture at large. He always was working slightly beyond the art world.


## DEREK ELLER

*Gallerist*

I'd gone to graduate school at the School of the Art Institute in Chicago, and afterward moved to New York. I got here in '93, and I probably started visiting Hudson's space then. I don't remember if everyone just knew Feature or if it was reading about the program in art magazines or the gallery guides that led me there. But it may have just been an awareness of the artists he was showing at that point. I was the kind of kid that as an undergraduate spent a lot of time in the library going through art magazines and looking at what was going on, and I remember feeling like, at least at the Green Street space, there was a lot happening there at once.

*You went to the School of the Art Institute to be an artist yourself?*

I did, yes. I have a studio degree from there. I was admitted into the photography department, but I made paintings the entire time. And I worked a lot with printmaking techniques, so I was using silk screen and photographic imagery and doing a lot of text-based work. But I stopped making art over twenty-five years ago. I basically just said, I'm done, and got this sort of crazy idea and opened a gallery.

Feature and Hudson are important to me personally. I feel like there haven't been that many galleries that I've really connected with, but I always had a strong affinity for Hudson and what he did. Because it seemed uniquely him and was so idiosyncratic and so stubborn in its own way. I never tried to emulate Hudson, but maybe he gave me that permission to feel comfortable being whatever I was going to be. I didn't love every show or every artist that he showed, but he was so ahead of the curve on a lot of things, and I was always interested to see what he was going to present. What he had to say through his choices. And I enjoyed his Q&As with artists.

I certainly got to know him a bit over the years. First of all, he had such an interesting and strong presence, I thought, within the physical space of the gallery, but then also in his taste. And his vision was always clear to me in the way that other galleries may show good art, but I'm not exactly sure what they're trying to do. They seem much more strategic or based on the marketplace. Hudson's operation always felt singular and personal, even though it was made up of so many different characters. You always felt like he really was sort of directing the whole thing. That was something that seemed apparent, even before I knew him. I was his neighbor on 25th Street, and I think the way he would be out there sweeping the sidewalk and washing the windows on a Saturday morning also said so much about the way he cared for his operation.

I opened in '97 and Hudson was one of my earliest customers. He came in and bought work and it was like a huge compliment to me. I mean, obviously to the artist too, but even to me as a dealer. He was always friendly and always respectful. Towards the end, he didn't come around as much anymore. But in the early years, I feel like he came to every show.

As far as other art dealers go, I always assumed he was very well respected. I'm always shocked today when speaking to a younger generation of people, I'll mention Feature Inc. and they'll just sort of look at me blankly. Or even actually earlier today, I was on the phone with an older artist and I mentioned Hudson and Feature, and he had no awareness of him. So these things always shock me. But most of the people in my immediate world certainly had a deep respect for him.

I think it was around '99 or 2000, I did a three-person show with Alex Ross, who was a Feature artist. Hudson was very helpful, generous, and easy to work with, but I remember he had such a unique style in terms of the way he would say, "Thank you for the ease of this transaction." Or address you in an email.

*"Hello Derek Eller…"*

Yes! [*laughs*] "Hello Derek Eller." Always your full name.

*In fact this book is titled* Hello *for that reason.*

I can tell you small things that have stuck with me for years. I remember once being in his space, and he was complaining about the walls not being plumb. And I might have said, well, it looks fine. He just looked at me. "The eye *knows*." It's so true, the eye does know. I also remember once we were walking down 25th Street together, and he said, "I have a rule. No pets, no plants."

*Do you think Feature could exist now?*

I don't know. I think there are many different ways to run a gallery. And maybe, again, as I was saying about permission, I feel like Hudson showed that you could run a gallery any way you wanted. But I don't think there will ever be another equivalent. There's nothing else that I've known or that's come after that's anything like it. And it's hard to even articulate why.


## NANCY SHAVER

*Artist*

I was trying to think of a few of my most important understandings that came from knowing Hudson. For one, the years at Feature were the beginning of understanding about how value of work, value of making, value of visual intelligence rarely, but occasionally, line up with market value. But those things are so separate. Hudson was very, very strong and good about keeping them separate. I've always felt like being with him all those years, regardless of what my work was perceived as, that I was incredibly intellectually well taken care of. What I know from him, what I intuited from him, and what I don't know but what I sensed, continues to grow in this really important way for me.

*When did you first become aware of him?*

I think it was 1986 or 1987. Hudson went to Kevin Larmon's apartment and saw an early work of mine that I'd given Kevin and responded to that. Then we had a short correspondence about it, and Hudson gave me my first gallery show in Chicago.

*A group show, and in less than a year you had a solo show there, and then others regularly. Were you actually represented by Feature then?*

No. I'm not sure of the date, but it was maybe 1999. I was very unhappy at my New York gallery, and felt like I was beginning to understand the art world in a way that made me realize how purely commercial it is. I called Hudson and asked him if he would take me on. He said he had to think about it. And then he called me a week later saying that he would. I remember that well, because I was driving to see Jackson, who is my husband now. It was a slippery icy day, and I rolled the car!

*Certainly a way to remember the day!*

I was just so happy. I'm a careful driver, but I was probably not paying attention to the fact of black ice at that point. [*laughs*]

*During these interviews I'm hearing that Feature provided an "oasis" for artists.*

I don't think I was fully aware of that when I was at Feature. But certainly since his death I am, totally. It's not like we had conversations or talks about the work in any way. There was intuition there. He was interested to believe in the work. I'm going to fast forward to my last meeting with him. They were always five-minute meetings. And I showed him some new things, and he said something like, "You know, Nancy, it's going to take a long time for your work to be seen and appreciated." Maybe not exactly what he said but that's what he meant. And god knows, that's the truth. It wasn't startling to me at the time, and I can now phrase it only in terms of what I know at the age of seventy-seven, and having been involved in the outskirts of the art world for maybe fifty years. And this is a phrase that I've only come up with after the last installation of a group endeavor that I'm now a part of: "Shows go up and they come down."

*It delighted him when you opened your shop Henry, in Hudson, New York. Did he ever come up to see Henry?*

He came once, very, very near the end. You know, there was never much time. So much was involved, and he was so busy. I don't really remember the visit much, but he seemed appreciative, and I was so happy that he came to see Henry.

*What were the pluses and minuses of working with a gallery that was run so differently than the majority of others?*

For me there weren't any difficulties with Hudson. Because I had such trust in him. Even if I didn't know exactly why he liked the work, I knew he was behind it, and that's all that sort of mattered. At his memorial I talked about that. He was fierce and intimidating, and I was mostly intimidated. But that didn't matter. I was willing to be intimidated, if that makes any sense. I believed so much in the honesty of his eye. And when I didn't understand it, which was often in terms of, say, his group shows and what he would put together, it would take a little while. There weren't the obvious connections of why this would be above that, but it was always incredibly important. I've come up with this other phrase, now being seventy-seven and having taught for twenty years—"how different visual intelligence is from book learning." And I think that's something that Hudson knew from the get-go. And relied on.

*It was a particular strength.*

Yes, his eye. And his willingness to take his time with that and to want to absorb intuitively before he got to the intellectual realm. In my studio I have that Judy Linn photograph of Hudson. That has always been incredibly important to me as a touchstone for what is important about this thing we call value, what's important about making, and what's important about seeing. The idea of being open and generous with all of those thoughts. And his absolute fierceness and his total respect for other human beings. And a kind of humor. A very good humor.

Thank you for asking me to do this. It was so valuable for me to think about Hudson this morning in a way that is directed. Because I think about him a lot, but it's just part of the atmosphere.


## ALEXANDER ROSS

*Artist*


I'd gone into the gallery way back in the early '90s and liked a lot of what I saw there. I didn't meet Hudson but I heard through the grapevine, "You know, he actually looks at slides. He doesn't just fold them up and send them back." This might have been 1991 or so. So I thought, well, why don't I send him some? And he responded. He said, "I'm interested. Let me come to your studio." So he did, and he was really brutally honest. But the fact that he even responded nicely, and then he came, blew my mind. He walked through my space and said, "You know, you have a lot of promise. But these over here are way too corny, and this over here is not working at all. I don't even know what *that* is. It doesn't look like the same artist made *these* things. But I see some talent. Send me some slides in a year or two." So that was like, oh wow, I have this goal and this vote of approval from some important guy. It really meant a lot. And I started to sort of think, this is his genius. Coming early and giving attention to people, to give them hope to rise to the occasion. So okay, I'm going to send slides to Hudson in a year and I'm gonna really try and make this work.

So I went to the gallery, I showed up to every opening. I looked at things. It was kind of a feedback loop. The kind of things that he was interested in showing started to become things I became interested in. There was still this sense of a vanguard, and he was clearly on it. Also, he was creating a gallery as a work of art. Which was intoxicating. I was younger, and everything was so hopeful.

So [over time] he would look at the slides and write back, saying, "It's getting better. Send more in a year." I finally left New York and went to the Catskills and really developed my thing. I came back and I had a studio on West 14th Street. This is five or six years later. When he came to that one he said, "You know what? You're ready." And he put me in a group show, and then things just took off. It was exhilarating, to say the least.

During that time there was so much money. He was selling things like crazy. I thought, "Oh yeah, this is working. I can quit my day job."

*All of that time may have forged a stronger connection with the work.*

Definitely. I perplexed him a little, because I was giving him a lot of different things. They were all under a clear umbrella, my ideas of the synthetic and the biological. But I would get graphic with some of the drawings. They would be going one way, painting would be going a different way. With collectors he told me, "A lot of times I just tell them that you like to play. That puts them at ease." Because there's something creepy about the work. So he would resort to that approach to describe what I was doing. But he himself would totally get into the science of it. And we were also both mesmerized and hypnotized by electronic music in the late '90s. It was dominating everything and was certainly influencing me. So that tapping into the technological side of my work, he got it completely.

*He was very strongly influenced by music.*

Early on I ran into him at a Guided By Voices concert. He was there by himself and I was there by myself. We noticed each other, and stood near each other in the loud music and just sort of waved. [*laughs*] So that opened up a dialogue. He started making me tapes, and I would make him tapes.

*I'm finding that he was friends with some of his artists, but had a more formal relationship with most.*

There was one time, right at the very beginning, that I happened to see him on Greene Street walking past. I said, "Hi Hudson," and he didn't even look at me or answer, he just kept walking. He was known to have this frosty side. But I was, "Well, you were just at my studio two weeks ago, and now you don't know me?" But then I remembered the voice of Bill Arning saying, "Develop a thick skin if you want to get anywhere in the art world." So I was, like, okay that's fine. He's busy, I get it. And I let it go. But I always knew that about him. He could suddenly turn a cold shoulder. I think it was just self-defense. He had to preserve his time and his energy and his mental space. But then when he *would* focus on you, it was like the sun. He would stare right into your eyes. So warm and accepting, listening. I felt like we were becoming friends but still keeping it cordial and businesslike, which is something I felt I needed to do. But he was so great, and you wanted to hang out with him and be friends with him. I didn't get close like some, but we were certainly sharing a lot of ideas. He would give me cultural things. He gave me a lot of written material, all these binders of esoteric information. This was before the internet. Hudson wouldn't commit. "I don't know if I believe this or don't believe this. It's just curious and fascinating. Check it out."

He said he was complaining about feeling dull and pressured, and he told me about cranial therapy. There was a certain doctor who would perform it, but it was sort of on the sly. He had to fly out to… I want to say, somewhere in northern California. He stayed there for a week and had a series of three treatments, where they inserted a very thick rubber balloon inside your sinus cavity, inflated it quickly to a certain pressure, and held it there. The balloon would push back on the skull and expand it a little, opening up fissures that fuse together when you are a baby. The idea was to push those open a little bit and give your brain more space. Which seems a little hard to accept scientifically, but when they finally deflated it he said he felt high, floating in the clouds for the next three days. He felt so completely refreshed and new and different. He was a new person. He gave me all this stuff to read about it. Some of it was really laughable, and some of it seemed serious and smart. I had both a big question mark about the whole thing and a fascination that on every level he was pushing boundaries.

*What do you think was the outside view of his place in the art world then?*

Not everyone in the art scene cared that much about Hudson. Certainly a lot of people did. Many artists and people who were interested in the new. But there are other issues in the marketplace obviously. Different levels and degrees of how much money people have, and what kind of operation they are running. So those coming from bigger concerns looked down on Hudson. Saw him as small, and saw him as a little whimsical. "Oh, it's cool. He's discovering new artists, running a nice service. But he's not the big time. He's staying small on purpose. And that's maybe a limitation of his," they might be thinking, or they might say to me. "It's a great gallery, but it's limited." I would hear that a lot. I think those limitations were intentional. I don't see why he would want to get big, because then it becomes something else.

*I'm wondering if he expected Feature to get as big as it even did.*

I wonder that too. I think he surprised himself. I'm betting. And then he realized what a great mind and eye he did have, and was able to build this impressive… one [artist] after another after another. It was his project, his wonderful, fruitful project. Why would he want to make it into a slick thing? I mean, he wouldn't do art fairs. And they became more and more important over time.

*His method began to get left behind.*

It was surprising to say, because he was so open-minded. But then, he was inflexible in some ways.

*You used the word "hopeful" earlier. Could that apply to the gallery itself?*

Absolutely. It was what is possible, and what is new. It was all about the feeling of newness. Like telling the world that the beginnings of a new portal are right here. Step through it with me, let me show you what I've found. The "zeitgeist" phenomenon is interesting to think about. Where is this stuff coming from? It's from all these little fountainheads that it's spraying out of. It moves around all the time, but he was on the nozzle big time. And for the most part he loved that role. "I know what's going on." And he did know.

## CARLO McCORMICK

*Critic and curator*

I think my first engagement with Hudson was that I really liked the work of Tony Tasset. But the thing was, I was really interested in one specific body of work, which had this kind of medical, um… tumescent fear. [*laughs*] Kind of like Cronenberg through the lens of AIDS. Tony had done a few pieces like that. But for Hudson it became a little bit of a thing because he wanted me to understand the entirety of his work, to make me understand the context of what Tony was up to as an artist. As long as I was willing to consider the entirety with the kind of intensity with which Hudson's gaze was penetrating, I didn't have to like it all. [*laughs*] We all do that. Hudson could still believe in someone, but then actively disagree on a body of work. His strength was that even though he was engaged in a conversation with everyone around him, it was very heavy on that love. You couldn't shrug, you had to thoroughly engage in whatever you were talking about.

Hudson was the only dealer that when you walked in the gallery, he was front and center. The only other guy I can think of was Richard Bellamy at Oil and Steel Gallery. He struck me as a relatively solitary guy who was really interested in a lot of things. I don't think I thought this at the time, but maybe in retrospect it was a little like those of us who worked in nightlife. Incredibly antisocial people thrust into a very social sphere. Most people who worked in clubs had a bar between them and everyone else. A DJ had a DJ booth away from the room. We wanted to be in the crowd but a little bit distanced from it. He seem to have the same kind of thing.

*As an art writer, what was your relationship? Were you wooed?*

He never really did that. Not much of a flatterer. So it sort of mystified me at the time. "Gee, why is Hudson nice to me? We don't agree on all that much." [*laughs*] I kind of would go in for a degree of seduction by art. That was a big difference between us. I think Hudson appreciated people who were smart and thinking about shit, and, as always, there were not that many around who were like that. As long as you were up to the rigor of this thinking, then he gave you a pass. He was actually quite generous that way. Though he could be cruel to those who didn't make that measure. He hated stupid artists.

*I'm trying to decide if he could flourish now.*

Hudson would have always cared about what he cared about, and the kind of thought process that he was involved in behind work. That work will always exist, and I think Hudson would continue. I never felt like alienation was particularly driving him the way it was some of us who had a more adversarial relationship to the mainstream of the market. I think that contributed to his great longevity within the art world. Most people, you either have your success or you fold your tent. He managed a kind of sustainability. That's not just a financial thing for most of us. More how do you keep your love for art when there are so many things about the art world that fucking piss you off? With Hudson it wasn't denial. He was very aware of everything he didn't like, but he had a persistence about what he cared about.

He did so much to remove his personality. Most people put their name on the shingle. It's sort of the identity of the dealer. He did a lot to avoid that, or even dismantle it. "We can talk about life in a minute, but let's talk about what we're looking at first." I didn't even know what his last name was. I don't think many people did.


## ANN BOBCO

*Friend*

The thing that struck me and remained with me is that Hudson was always an artist in his own right. Yes, he ran a gallery, but he did not want—and he did not take—economic support and guidance from other people. Nor did he enjoy the socializing with people in institutions who might otherwise benefit his artists. So there was in essence, to my mind, a purity about Feature. But it was also a very frustrating place for artists who wanted to grow. I say this because of my particular involvement with Bill [Wurtz], who was making art that was not very accessible for a long time. Hudson was not able to sell much of his work, but supported Bill for many years anyway. It was my take that Hudson always was able to support Feature through secondary sales. I have to say, I really admired that. Because I continued to have so many issues with the art world as it was, and is.

I think that he was such an interesting combination of the sacred and profane. A person who truly believed and was truly skeptical. He had such an incredible work ethic through, I'm sure, his family structure. And then this rebellious streak. He was such a rich individual who, madly, was very human. He had the effect, for many of us, as being one of the most sincere people possible, but then there was this side to him that really did not want to be transparent.

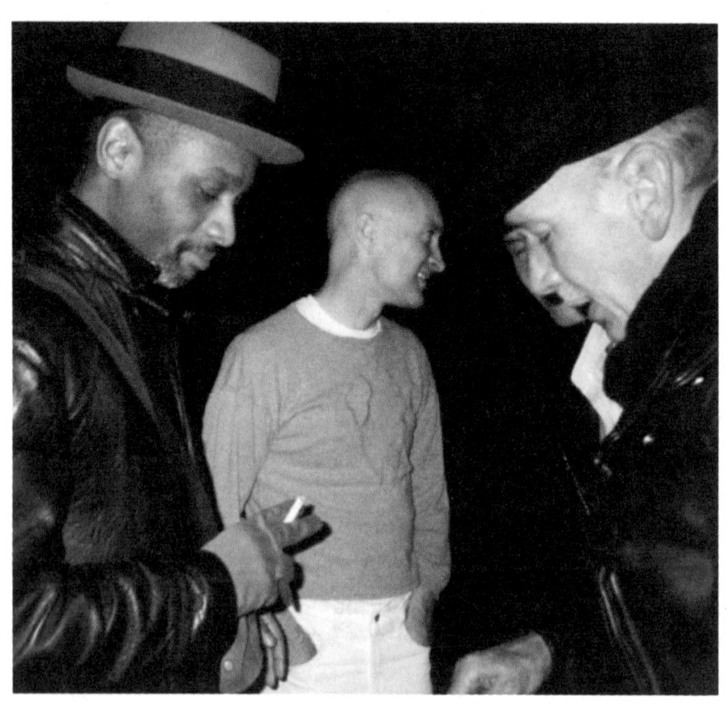

Jack Walls, Hudson, unknown, and Rosa von Praunheim, New York City, 1996.
Photo: Steve Lafreniere

He was aware of having an echo chamber effect. I remember when I first knew him in the early '80s, him saying that the thing about being an artist is that you put these ideas into the world and it doesn't matter *how* you inoculate it. Sometimes it's a lie, or you overdo things. All that matters is the effect they have.

*You went on to design some Feature catalogs.*

In the middle of Hudson's health crisis I pulled together the Tom Friedman catalog, *0202*. It was a really interesting experience for me because, as we know, to say that Hudson was a micromanager is to minimize his need for control. So I never had contact with Tom, which is a really interesting thing as an art director and a designer. But it worked just fine.

*Well, let's talk about the health crisis you mentioned. He was HIV-positive, so there was a lot of speculation that it was AIDS.*

I want to say it was September of 2003. Leading up to what happened, he'd had a really intense… it was a pustule on his head. He had also been acting all out of sorts. Some of us were fearful that it might be some kind of brain cancer. Then I think that started to heal up. What I remember happening was that at a certain point someone from the gallery called Bill and said, "You know, Hudson's not really feeling well. Would you be willing to come over to his apartment and make a meal for him, or sit with him?" So Bill did, and it seemed clear that Hudson really wasn't well. And then the next day or two, someone else asked me, "Ann, would you mind making him some…" because I was really into making borscht. [*laughs*] Which ended up being my job in all this. Then [his gallery assistant] Anne Doran got pulled in, and then David Shaw. It ended up being, for a week or so, that we were all going over in shifts to his apartment and helping to take care of him.

He was becoming less and less able to be responsive. This was a person that I cared about, and I had no qualms about doing whatever was needed to be done. But that was when it really hit me, that this was serious. Because I think Hudson was still in his very disciplined and delusional state, thinking that he was just going to pull through.

*Acting as if he just had the flu.*

Yeah. So then I think it was just one of those things where somebody said, "You have got to go to the hospital." And so he did. As for me, for the next two months I was on breakfast patrol. I would bring him his breakfast, Bill would bring him his lunch. Anne Doran would maybe bring him dinner.

He was there for quite a while. He kept the gallery humming along as best he could from a hospital bed, but it really dragged on him. One of the things that was most striking to me was when maybe he'd been in there for a month or so. I was alone with him, after the breakfast patrol. There was no nurse around. He seemed very despondent. Until that point he hadn't gotten really down. But he was in this place of saying how he just felt like he had given everything away, and that he didn't want to live. I don't know, it half made me really sad and half pissed me off. So, in my way of dealing with things, I just started crying. I said, "You know, you're entitled to whatever you're going through, but it sounds like you should hang in there!" And it was one of those things where, for all of us, we never know where the recognition of our humanity in whatever form will somehow rally us. But it seemed after that—and not necessarily just from what I said—he realized, okay, he was going to give it one more try. And it was also because of those un-fucking-believable nurses—they were just outrageously good—and of course in some ways he charmed them. When he got out he sent them all checks privately, to show his appreciation.

What I remember is that he was told at the hospital that his very exacting vegetarian diet, and his being so thin from it, wasn't a great match with an HIV-positive status. He didn't like hearing that, and told them so. The infection he had was minor, but was being severely aggravated by his compromised immune system. When he finally left the hospital, re-modelers were working at his apartment, so he rented a townhouse off of Houston Street on Mulberry. I was duly enrolled to help out there a few hours a day. I prepared his meals, and that's when he started eating meat again. I'd known him for twenty years and had never seen that before. I think he decided that he needed some animal protein.

## SAM GORDON

*Artist and gallerist*

I moved to New York in 1996 and saw shows in SoHo consistently to figure out where it might make sense to show my work. I knew of Feature before, then started seeing every show. That fall I asked Hudson if he was look-ing at slides. He did have an open viewing policy October/November and April/May when he would accept submissions and write his famous notes.

My first show of drawings and photographs was in May 1997, paired with an exhibition from the estate of Candy Darling. I worked with Feature from 1997 through 2014.

*How would you describe the rigor that Hudson imposed on the gallery, and his expectations of the workers and artists?*

That dichotomy makes me laugh, because yes there was a silence im-posed, like monks in a monastery, worker bees going about business. But Hudson gave me space, the freedom to do whatever I wanted. When we screened my video project "The Lost Kinetic World" in 2007, he and Anne Doran couldn't watch the video from their desks, only hear it. The video has all these "art moments" captured with so many different sounds. One thing they laughed about was the disembodied voice of Justin Vivian Bond reading Valerie Solanas' SCUM Manifesto being accompanied by Matmos. Just another day at work. Anne helped edit the full list of artists included in the project, Carl Ferrero helped lay out the booklet. Hudson sent them out to his mailing list. I only realized in retrospect, the video was a movie as a magazine, and must have reminded Hudson of *Farm*, a continuation of sorts, and an opportunity to share one of his classic cards, "'With Compliments—Hudson.'"

*As co-owner of a gallery, you're still very much in the art world. How do Hudson and your years showing at Feature affect your own space?*

Definitely somehow. Through osmosis over sixteen years? I was fortunate to have two great mentors, Hudson and Bob Gober, who I worked for. Bob bought some of the great Tom of Finland preparatory drawings from Feature in the '90s. For Hudson, be it Tom or Tantra or Korwa drawings, there were no hierarchies. Raymond Petttibon is to punk as Tabboo!, who we show, is to queer—the visual language. So perhaps comparisons can be made between Feature Inc. and Gordon Robichaux? Jacob Robichaux, my partner in the gallery, as an artist and art advisor knew Hudson, did some business with him. He acquired a Vince Fecteau. I have an early Fecteau through Hudson too. So, yes, there are many small connections. We are also artist advocates, we pay artists first, we have no debt. We do refer sometimes to our "GR family." Hudson had "Feature Creatures." Hopefully, any good gallery forms a community, a context for the artists.

Hudson always swam against the tide, despite showing Richard Prince, Jeff Koons, Charles Ray, Sarah Charlesworth, Kay Rosen, Lily van der Stokker, Huma Bhabba, Nancy Shaver, Judy Linn, Tom Friedman, Richard Hawkins, B. Wurtz, David Robbins! Conversely some of the most vulnerable artists, whose legacies during the AIDS crisis would have otherwise been lost, such as Arnold Fern, Jochen Klein, and Rene Santos, were championed by Hudson. "AIDS is not over" has become a rally call for the work still to be done.

He was so many things, so many stories. I'm thinking about the fantastic Jim Shaw portrait of Hudson made of bubble gum, photographed brand new and then again years later for archiving or insurance, half the bubble gum eroded, ravaged like it was Hudson's very own portrait of Dorian Gray. Those "healing machines" that he showed by The Gentle Wind Project. The incense evening with a smelling, like a tasting, though a lecture/performance, and then dinner for all at the Savoy in SoHo. That also turned out to be the day of Hudson's birthday, though he didn't mention it. Hudson is legendary, so we do hope our experiences with him reverberate through what we do [in our gallery].

With art world amnesia, so many people don't even know who he or Feature Inc. was. It can be heartbreaking. Though for those that do know—that were either there, remember, heard, or have learned since—they all respond with a kind of reverence usually reserved for saints and martyrs. But what he did is possible now. There are great artist-run galleries in business today, and Feature was very much that. Maybe, in retrospect, Hudson is a cautionary tale of what not to do—his interests lay more in the discovery than in the career. He helped to mint artists. There are many that carry on the spirit of his legacy through the interesting, devotional work they do in support of artists, and I see Hudson's artists everywhere, all the time. That's his legacy too.

He was also great about donating work to museums. He gave two of my drawings to the Walker. Two summers ago I donated my G.B. Jones drawing I bought from him, to the Tang in his honor.

*It has to be said how much he loathed what the art world was becoming in his later years. Was that ever a subject that you remember discussing with him?*

Seems many have a love/hate relationship with the art world. Hudson had deep connections with artists, and collectors like Eileen Cohen, who was invested in the gallery's program and offered support to Feature at critical junctures. Hudson participated in the relaunch of the Armory Fair in 2000, and seemed to hate being there, so he dropped out of the fair ecosystem during the next ten years while it became the dominant portal for new collectors. When he did get back to fairs—Independent, NADA, Outsider Art Fair—I would see some collectors walk right past his booth, not familiar with Feature's program. Even in the late '90s though, at a Dennis Cooper reading, I remember talking with Hudson about this topic. The "cred versus income" disparity was always there, and as the art world became over-professionalized and hyper-commercialized, Hudson stuck to his own interests. The art-industrial-complex continues to grind forward. I feel he did loathe it, though he never stopped laughing at it too. He knew what was real.


## LILY VAN DER STOKKER

*Artist*

I had owned my own art gallery on the Lower East Side from '83 to '86. My neighbor was Colin de Land. Of course I knew him a bit, and I was looking up to him because he was so cool and his art shows were so terrific. At some point after I closed my gallery in the late '80s, I was in New York, making my art, thinking maybe I should try and find a gallerist. Since I knew Colin from 6th Street, that could be easy. I could just ask to show him my work. So I sat at his table and showed him my little paintings on canvas. At that time I had painted the word "Good" as a sort of signature on all my artworks. He said, "Good?" That was an interesting moment. Nothing came out of it.

Not much later a friend from the Netherlands who had met Hudson and had talked to him about my work said maybe I should go talk to him. [My partner] Jack and I had seen several exhibitions at Hudson's new space on Broome Street. Jack and I would see all of the new art shows in New York at that time, and we saw this new gallery Feature, and we liked it. Now, since I had my own gallery, and I was used to artists bringing me slides all the time, I felt, hmmm, I don't want to do that. I knew how uninteresting those can be. A guy one time brought a stone sculpture into my gallery on a two-wheeler and rolled it right in front of my desk. So I didn't want to do that either. [*laughs*] So I just made color Xeroxes of my drawings. Like fifty, and I brought those to Feature. Jim took them. He was very friendly. He said, "We will look at them and you can pick them up next week." So that was easy.

*In your book* How I Went to New York *you describe not having representation until 1989, when you dropped off those photocopies. You wrote: "A week later I went back and Hudson had written a letter about my work. It said: 'The work is clunky, stupid, humorous, pretty, mundane, personalised.' Hudson had prepared me before he gave me the letter, saying that those were compliments... He said he wanted to do a studio visit soon."*

Yes. This was a special moment I had with him. He gave me the letter with a naughty smile. But the words that he used, because me being from The Netherlands my English was not that good, so I had to look some of the words up in a dictionary to see what he meant by it. So yes, this was funny. And so typically Hudson. Because he was always playing with words with me. About art and content, superficial and deep at the same time. I liked it.

*Someone described one side of him as grinning Buddhist monk.*

Oh yes. With a little mean streak here and there. And also lots of love for your art. He had such enormous love for every detail of your work. And he seemed to really understand deep into the heart of what you were doing, as nobody else did. But this I only found out a little later, after we did several studio visits. At first it was all quite new and exciting to meet him. I really had the feeling that I had won the lottery. Good things only happen a few times in your life, if they happen, and this was definitely one of those. Meeting Hudson was a special important moment in my life.

*Can you contrast that experience with other galleries?*

Well, looking back now, all of my galleries are special in their own way. Over the years they have become like family, like my best friends. My other galleries also have special ways of understanding my art, which is wonderful. I'm older now, so most galleries I worked with I've known for twenty or thirty years.

Hudson was regarded as my most important gallery at the time by the other galleries. Over the years I developed with my other four galleries also special relationships. Good and fair business people, most of them. But like with Hudson, my wall paintings are not easy to sell. So you have to have a certain type of gallerist who is really into your art.

*He supported the wall drawings early on?*

Yes. My first wall painting I made in Feature in 1990. Not my very, very first one, but the history of my wall painting artist life started then, when I made my "Friendly Good" wall painting at Feature on Broome Street. When Hudson saw it happening, standing behind me while painting he said, "You are going to make a lot of wall paintings!" It sounded like an incantation. And he was right, this was definitely the beginning of my wall paintings. And he totally encouraged me making wall paintings for my second solo exhibition with him in 1992. He provided me with an assistant and a space where I could prepare the wall painting papers real-size to transfer on the Feature walls, a complex method. Later I used a slide projector. So he definitely encouraged me to do three more wall paintings for the second solo show in 1992. Then things really seemed to start. I remember a friend coming to my opening and saying, "Lily, there's a buzz around your work," and it was a very crowded opening. So yes, Hudson had a vision about how he wanted to stimulate you as an artist and your art to grow.

*Having owned a gallery yourself, what did you find significantly different about Feature's shows?*

For one, he was gay. He showed Tom of Finland and Arnold Fern. And it was not so aggressive—Feature had a very different look. No hiding behind a desk in back. And at openings, no beer and wine, but pear juice and cookies. That was different too. Also, in that time I was speaking regularly with an artist friend who kept saying to me, "Oh, I wish I worked with Hudson. Feature is really an artists' art gallery, can you please introduce me?" Hudson was working very hard selling the art, but it was certainly an artist-friendly gallery.

Now, when I was in the Netherlands with other artists and I wanted to brag about being with Hudson, they were never very impressed. And I was thinking, why not? I'm with the best gallery that you can think of in New York. But they were looking at Sonnabend or Paula Cooper. Those were good galleries, but not Hudson or Feature, no. But most artists in New York, they knew how good he was. Something else I want to point out is that Hudson was sometimes making shows and I would be thinking, "Wow, this is really Hudson." In those days I was stepping away from modernism, and I was adventuring into the decorative. I felt Hudson and I were on a similar path, and he was making shows that were so different from anything else you saw. Like making a show about the curl: *Arabesque*. One time he made a weird but cool exhibition showing paintings from these people—I can't remember the name—but you had to sit down and touch the paintings on a table and meditate? That last thing I forgot. But the touching was something.

At first he did sell my drawings. They were selling for very little money then. Each time I would come back to New York [from the Netherlands] Hudson had sold a few drawings, and I'd get $700. I could buy my food for that so I was quite happy. I didn't have to bring money from the Netherlands. This is how I started to live on the sales of my art. But later on, the bigger work, the wall paintings, would never sell. I don't blame him for it because they only sometimes sold one every few years, mostly to a museum. But I think in my later shows he was getting frustrated about that. I noticed because I had a solo show, and he said, "Let's just not put a price with it because we're not going to sell these anyway."To me, it didn't sound so nice. My first concern was always content and the realization of the works on location. Selling was not my primary goal. So I myself was never so disappointed about it.

But I must say, at the very end of me and Hudson, he did a few things that were not very honest. He said that he would always sell with a 10 percent discount, and then I found out at some point that he kept the discount for himself. Because he sold to my friends sometimes and I asked them did you get a discount? And they said no. But Hudson would charge me the discount, so that was not so… And Hudson I trusted like nobody else, so that hurt me. That was painful. But he had to survive with his gallery, he had to sell. Nevertheless I think his main passion always was the art.

*This changed your relationship.*

In the last years I was getting a bit scared of him. You would enter the gallery and then go sit at his desk. You had some things to ask about or discuss. You would put your bag on the floor next to you, but he would say, "No, the bag has to go over there." Some spot he had reserved out of the view of the visitor. He was so peculiar about how you had to behave in his office. It made me feel uncomfortable. So he was getting more and more a control person. He was sort of a lion on his mountain. The fun was gone.

*There's a funny section in your book where you talk about seeing Hudson out one day and how sexy he was.*

Yeah! It's really true. The story was that one day Jack and I saw him walking on the opposite side of the street on Wooster Street. We waved at him. And we were looking at him and thinking wow. Jack said to me, "He's a looker." He had to explain to me what the word means. [*laughs*] Hudson was wearing his beige cowboy jacket with fringe on it. He walked straight up with such confidence, and looked so smart and happy. We knew that he had an active sex life, and we thought, oh, he must be on his way to another good-looking man. This was in the first years that I met him, 1991 or '92. Much later in the 2000s, he got sick and he got all these difficulties with his body, and this is when he was growing this peculiar typical Hudson beard thing. A different look, also good. And he always wore these nice red-and-yellow-colored embroidered shirts that he bought from a small design store on Avenue A. But then because of his sickness, his life was getting tough. And working with him was getting tough as well. Everything was. You could see that he had a really hard time. So then the sexy part I didn't see anymore.

When he threw me out of the gallery, or… I left the gallery in 2003, that was quite painful for me. But in a way, I think Hudson and I really loved each other. I remember coming back to Feature openings, and each time I wouldn't behave like an artist that was hurt, because I was still so happy and connected to the Feature family. So each time when I saw Hudson, I would just smile and joke. I couldn't find another gallery at that time, but I would still always be kind and positive to him. Probably also because the difficulties of working together were behind me. And then I found a new gallerist in New York. Hudson even came to my opening dinner.

*You remained friends.*

Oh yes. One time Hudson and I went out to have a meal in a Lower East Side restaurant. He was really kind and we were joking. We discussed about getting older and what to do about old age. If we would always be doing art or not. He was saying, "Maybe I want to go live outside of the city." And then suddenly he said, "Lily! We could get married." I said, "Yes, we could." [*laughs*] He said, "Then you could have a green card and you could come to the United States. And I could go to Europe!"

*There you go.*

Then four months later he died. But I must say, I had this nice dinner in my memory. I still see his happy face. It was a good last meeting.

# NATHANIEL ROBINSON

*Artist*

I worked at Feature from 2005 onward. I finished grad school at the School of the Art Institute in Chicago, where I had studied with Richard Rezac. When I was going to New York he sort of set me up with a meeting at Feature, which got me the job. But I didn't know very much when I went in there and talked to Hudson for the first time. I was hired for the position of "Eyes," to do with the slides. And I remember another position there was called "Hands," and that was the registrar. Anne [Doran] was "Editor."

*You arrived during its sizable Chelsea incarnation on West 25th Street.*

There was a strangely domestic feel to the space, in combination with a really ascetic, almost clinical quality. That was kind of striking. It seemed personal and idiosyncratic, but there were aspects of it that were aspiring to some sort of neutrality and blankness. Polar opposites at the same time. Those qualities about it stuck with me and still ring true, knowing what I know now. And I got the sense that people paid attention to what happened there. There was every expectation that something important could happen at Feature at any moment. [*laughs*] So it was maybe all the more remarkable that Hudson did strange, incomprehensible things that people might not have agreed with.

*Can you give an example?*

Off the top of my head, I remember him doing a show of artifacts that were supposed to be healing devices. I think they were made basically by a cult. I thought that was pretty impressive. I was probably more interested at that time than I am now in alternate, parallel art worlds. Different regimes of aesthetics and stuff like that. So the idea that this community was making things by their own lights, and then that got transplanted into the middle of the mainstream art scene was interesting to me. And I guess he did that in a few ways. But it had an edge to it that galleries bringing in "outsider" artists don't have. There was potentially something objectionable here, and something very alien and possibly dangerous. There was a definite, functional purpose to these things which was also really dubious.

I didn't pay that much attention to how it was talked about, and there wasn't really social media then, but somehow I got the sense that some people thought it wasn't a good use of the precious time and space that could instead be devoted to worthwhile art. But that was an aspect of Hudson that was a little frustrating, that he sometimes seemed to go beyond just an interest in things and go ahead and believe in them.

*I found over time that what appeared to be his forays into being a true believer were usually about only certain aspects of the thing at hand. He wanted to get closer to those ideas, so walked right up to see how they worked. Do other things stand out about working so closely with him?*

I think of contradictions. Like, there was an open and egalitarian aspect to the relationship between him and the personnel there. And yet he was also kind of an autocrat, probably for good, for the best. Because that gave it its specificity, in terms of the personality behind it. I didn't have any qualms about trying my best to do things the way he wanted them done, because I figured it was his show. And I also wasn't some kind of credentialed expert in the job I was doing. I was invested in trying to be competent at it and making things go as smoothly as I could. And Hudson may have sought out people like that, whose self image didn't create friction with their duties at the gallery. It's interesting in retrospect, why did he think I'd be a good person for this? One thing I sort of regret sometimes is that he once asked me if I was interested in thinking about curating anything. And I basically said no, and that timewise I couldn't get done what I wanted to in the studio as it was. That's what my life was about. That was pretty stupid, I think. I probably should've seen at least what he was getting at.

*Not a lot of galleries make that sort of offer to the assistants. Did he seem interested in your work?*

Well, my other relationship with him, and maybe the more important one, was as an artist. He was generous about studio visits. He seemed to be able to gauge people's personalities and what they wanted or needed from him. In my case he kind of left me alone. In retrospect that's a miraculous amount of trust that he put in me. At one point he asked me to do a [solo] show and set a date, and then basically let me do what I wanted to do. And then he didn't ask me about it again until he became a little frustrated a couple of days before the opening and said, "I kind of have to know what you're doing." He also did a lot to enable my crazy ideas, especially since the gallery was diminished in scale at that point. This was at Allen Street. He let me hang this inverted fountain piece. A big object hung from the ceiling, which I didn't really know how to do! Maybe the way that I related to him and that he related to me was that he was just going to enable whatever idea I had, and there wasn't any sense of trade off or compromise. In the end I think that gave me an unrealistic idea of what a gallery is, as an artist.

*Hudson had a bad feeling about the direction the art business was moving in those last years.*

The art world was merging with other regimes, like advertising and fashion. Money was taking over. Other than that I can't myself pinpoint what the change was and what his problem was with it. I know he was very reluctantly starting to have a presence at art fairs. He told me he would be sitting there and people would pass by saying, "Hey, you're a legend!" [*laughs*] But they wouldn't buy anything. I think he just felt he had a responsibility to the artists, so he tried to do fairs, and make money doing some secondary market stuff. So he wasn't totally resisting.

There was this idea afoot to do some kind of benefit for him and Feature. I don't think he really liked the idea. It was a commercial gallery. He had a history of working with non-profits early on, so he saw the distinction between what he was doing with Feature and a gallery that would be a candidate for something like that. So he somehow morphed that idea into doing this show called *Power to the People* where he had everyone, from high profile artists to just anyone who wanted to contribute something, cover the walls, and on the appointed day anyone could come and take anything. And that was his idea of a benefit, giving things away. It was so funny. A comic inversion of a benefit.

## STEEL STILLMAN

*Artist and writer*

*On May 1, 2010, Feature was the site of a somewhat radical art world event.*

*Power to the People* was an exhibition that looked like a benefit but wasn't one at all. Instead, 263 artists, many of whom were quite well known, offered Hudson work for a one-day show in which everything was given away. No money changed hands.

*What led up to it?*

Its roots were in Feature's departure from Chelsea, two years earlier. The gallery's lease there was ending, and Hudson, feeling Chelsea had become too corporate, was eager to try something new. He set his sights on a big new space on the Bowery and then, sadly, got caught up in an expensive and complicated renovation. Just when the new space was ready to open, the global financial system collapsed.

*The September 2008 stock market crash happened the very week the Bowery gallery opened. It was terrible timing.*

It was. At the time, Hudson was still wrangling with contractors' bills and the city's building department, which hadn't yet signed off on the renovation, and nobody was buying art. By the following June, he couldn't keep the doors open and closed the gallery. Of course, Hudson and everyone around him were devastated. Ironically, the New Museum had recently reopened a block away. Had the Bowery version of Feature survived, it would have held a prominent place in the emerging Lower East Side scene.

*Is that when the idea of putting together a benefit show arose?*

Right. In the summer and fall of 2009, when it wasn't clear whether the gallery would reopen, various people—current and former Feature artists and other art world friends—tried to persuade Hudson to do a benefit to get the gallery back on its feet. But he resisted, saying that benefits were for nonprofits. He had worked in the nonprofit world and was determined that Feature never be considered in that light. Luckily though, by December, Hudson's precarious finances began to stabilize, and he reopened the gallery on Allen Street, in a more modest storefront.

*No need for a benefit.*

Hudson was relieved that a benefit hadn't been necessary, but he was enormously touched that so many artists, including artists with no real connection to the gallery, had offered to help. So he decided to turn the art community's offer of support back to those who had offered it, and to the public at large. Hudson believed that art was about the transfer of experiences and ideas through the vehicle of artworks. It was that transfer, more than the objects themselves, that mattered. What could be better than letting that happen for free.

Power to the People *happened on May Day, and there was a queue down Allen Street to get in. I know you donated work. Were you there?*

I was. It was festive and kind of chaotic. Many people knew one another, of course, and everyone was scurrying around trying to decide what they wanted. Nothing was identified. All the work was displayed in clear plastic bags, pinned to the wall. If you liked a piece, you took it. One to a customer. Hudson or someone was keeping a list of who got what at the door. Staging *Power to the People* on May Day was certainly symbolic—an echo of the first Feature having opened in Chicago in 1984 on April Fools' Day. Not only was the gallery back on its feet, but it was hosting a celebration of art-worker spirit and community. Though he had staged it, Hudson was emphatic that the show had been made by us, for us.

*It must have left a kind of glow.*

It made a big impression on me, and on a lot of people. It was yet another indication that Hudson's art-first, business-second approach to being a gallerist was at the same time a critique of the art system. He accepted being part of the art world, but insisted on his own rules and, for the most part, got away with it. But reflecting now on *Power to the People*, something else occurs to me that you might appreciate, having known Hudson in Chicago, when he was still a performance artist. *Power to the People* may well have been Hudson's last great performance piece. And we were all so lucky to have been part of it.

*I like that idea. The profile of Hudson you later wrote for* Art in America *in 2010 used* Power to the People *to introduce his sensibility.*

The contrarian nature of *Power to the People* was what convinced my editor to let me do the piece. And my conversations with Hudson opened his world to me in ways I remain grateful for. He was immensely candid about his own history as an artist and performer, and about the history of the gallery and his relationships with the art world. Those talks were a kind of master class, and I learned a lot.

*Preparing for this interview, last week I sent you a few of his quotes from that article. I thought we could talk about them. Here's the first:*

I firmly believe that viewers or collectors should go to the art. Art should not be delivered to them. I'm always amused to hear dealers

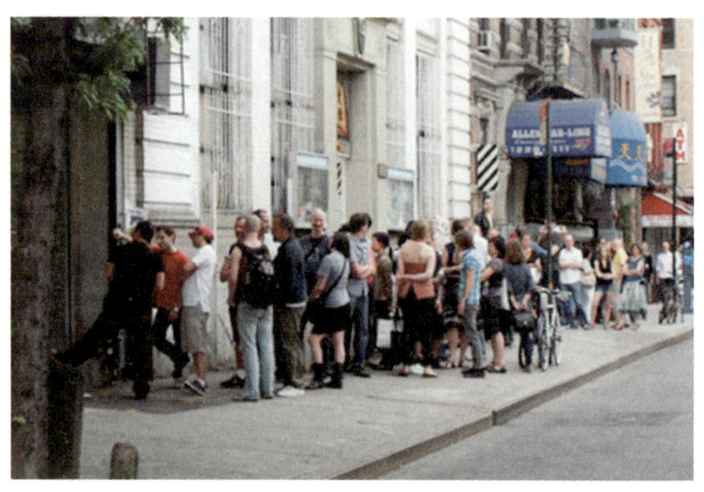

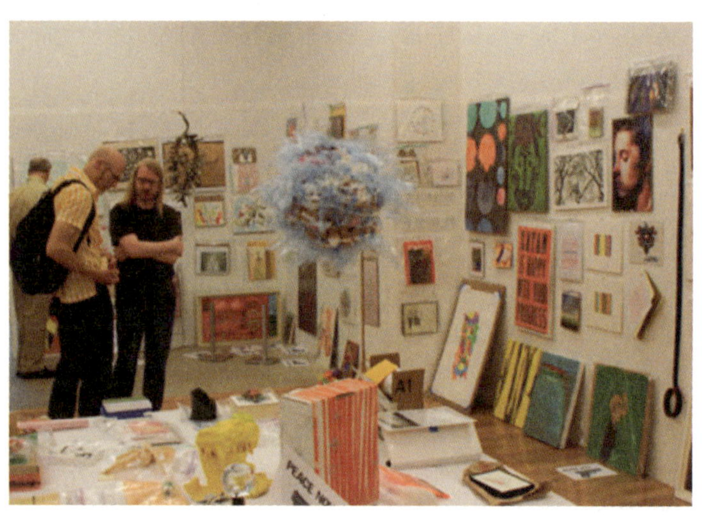

*Power to the People*, Allen Street, New York City, May 1, 2010. Photos: Avi Adler

talking up clients by telling them about an artist's upcoming exhibitions, inclusion in noted private or museum collections and so on—as if those things really make an artist or artwork better. Why isn't the bullshit of that house of cards transparent to listeners? It's far too rare that you hear someone speaking about how an artwork expresses itself; about what is inventive or engaging in the artist's use of materials; or about how the content impacts your thinking or emotional life.

That summarizes Hudson's difference from the entire art world apparatus—which includes not just galleries and museums and auctions and art fairs but also MFA programs and the art media. In many ways he was a purist who wanted to preserve experiences of looking at and understanding and making art from the distortions of the art system. He knew he was fighting a losing battle and that art in capitalist contexts would always face those kinds of headwinds, but that didn't mean people should lose sight of what mattered most. At the same time, Hudson was an optimist who believed in art's agency, in its power to resist society's misuses and misunderstandings. In the *Art in America* piece, he tells the story of an artist friend, doing a job in the home of some wealthy art collectors, who asked the wife how long it had taken them to build their collection. She said they'd bought it all the previous year, clearly with the help of an art advisor. Hudson went on to say:

At first I was horrified, but then it dawned on me that the art might yet have the last word. When you live with art—once your initial interactions fade—a kind of osmosis takes over, and you absorb all kinds of things just by being in its proximity. You may not be paying attention to it, but it is paying attention to you.

*This connects to another quote from your piece where Hudson describes his way of approaching an artwork:*

The first thing is to be quiet, to drop my agenda or expectations, and listen. Then I soften my gaze. The eyes are aggressive, and once you realize they're out there hunting, you can learn to tune them down and let what is out there come to you. The body knows things way before the brain does.

I love this idea of softening the gaze. Of lowering the volume of one's inner monologue—all that chatter of art criticism and self—and opening to whatever's in front of you. It's a phrase and approach I share often with friends and students and try to practice myself in galleries, museums, and other people's studios. Hudson loved having silent one-on-one viewing sessions with artworks, and his description of these sessions reminded me of meditation practices. He believed that making and viewing art was about developing consciousness, not about making or possessing art objects. The artwork was, in his words, "just a catalyst."

*Hudson uses that phrase "just a catalyst" twice in your article. And both times it suggests that he had a mediumistic view of what an artwork is.*

Yes, the second time he uses the phrase—in a description of an Alice Coltrane performance with the Yale Symphony Orchestra he'd seen in the late '60s or early '70s—is from the original, unpublished version of the *Art in America* piece:

> It wasn't long after her husband's death. In the middle of a piece, she just lost it, and burst into tears. They had to carry her offstage. But it was the most amazing experience—seeing an artist really go. That is the sense you get when artists become fully transparent to their work. […] The person transmutes into the object, and the object transmutes into me, as viewer. The development of the person, not the development of the object, makes that happen. The object is just a catalyst.

In my view, Hudson was as interested in people as he was in art. And there was something of a teacher in him that had its roots in his own early education, when, in fifth grade, he was invited to teach art to special education students several years older than he was. Indeed, there were many people in the Feature orbit who thought of him as a kind of teacher or guru.

*Sure, somewhere between nurturing and pedantic.*

As a teacher, he wasn't interested in getting anybody from point A to point B, or in making them into something they weren't. His mode was more progressive, more about bringing things out of people, than putting things in. He was skeptical and dismissive of a lot of what happens in art schools, especially in the aftermath of the '80s obsession with theory. He felt all of that just confused people and put students in the position of believing they needed theoretical handholds, when what they really needed was to go deeper into who they were and what they were seeing.

*Continuing with this notion of the artist's perspective, the final quote I have is from the end of your piece. In it, Hudson says that for an artist to make a work is to make a picture:*

> The picture is of something inside them, or a response to something in the world. To do either is everything. Art-making is an old form, and that's important to remember when you get involved with the art world. Making a picture (or a thing) and looking at a picture (or a thing) are quite primitive, primal experiences—and they remain so despite all our technologies and ideas.

A picture, whether a view of the world or an image, is an idea, perhaps beyond language. Artists all have ways of thinking, ideas that become manifest in artworks. The ideas may be inchoate and wordless, but they develop and grow as you work, as the picture inside you changes and clarifies. In literature, before it became fashionable to believe the author was dead, people would talk about the writer's voice, and I think that's close to what Hudson had in mind.

# KIM REINHARDT and ANDREW ZAROU

*Artists*

Andrew: My initial awareness of Feature was circa 2000. One of the closest connections was the artist Arturo Herrera. At the time he was in the city and he was kind of a mentor to me. He was the first person to talk to me directly about Feature. He said something along the lines of, "You may not like the work. But it always makes you think." He had a certain kind of affinity or reverence for Hudson as a thinker, an entity in the art world. It put a spark in my head, like, oh, that's a place that needs to be on my map.

I had laid eyes on Hudson in person going into the gallery, but I found him intimidating, just visually. A lot of that had to do with [*laughs*] his really long, sharp sideburns. Plus, somebody like Arturo, who I had a lot of respect for, kind of put him on a pedestal in a sense, so… I rendered him unapproachable. But I went to the gallery anyway, and I was intrigued. Some of the earliest things I remember seeing were paintings by Mamie Holst. I felt that it was work that I equally understood and I had questions about.

My connection with him interpersonally really started with him putting feelers out for somebody to help with the gallery, installing. A mutual friend, Joan Weakley, recommended me. And so in 2010 I did some freelance for him. Hudson offered me a position, but I begged off for various reasons. I think really it was incompatible with my other freelance work, which was with museums. And then I remember talking to a friend of mine about not wanting to work for a gallery that you might want to show with, because then you're kind of seen in that role and that role only. I talked about this years later with Joan, and she said, "Well, that makes sense for a lot of places, except for Feature. Because look at Nathaniel [Robinson]." Hudson seemed to be inclusive toward the work he liked, it didn't matter if you worked for him or not. After I installed the Jonathan Hartshorn show in 2010 he invited me to come back and take one piece for free, which was unexpected and really cool. I was thinking, this is not normal Chelsea [*laughs*] and trying to understand the Hudson/Feature ethos. It was kind of a non-commercial/commercial entity.

Kim: I first met Hudson in 2012. He and Andrew arranged for us and some others to attend an Earth show at Littlefield [*Brooklyn live music venue*]. I had a vague idea that he had a gallery, and that he was a good person. I also knew that he was interested in yoga, and at the time I was practicing Ashtanga, so I tried to talk to him a little about that. The next time I talked to him was at Feature, the *Amo Legomandala* show [by Kylin] in 2013.

Andrew: I was waiting for Kim to arrive. I didn't want to come off as this gallery stalker so I just sat down in a corner discreetly. The next thing, he sat down next to me. "How's it going, Mr. Z?"

Kim: I feel like I'm one of those people who can easily feel people's energy and vibes, and he stood out for me exceptionally at the Earth show. I just remember him kind of circling the room, and my being very aware of his presence. At the *Legomandala* show, Andrew had a laptop with him, and I guess Hudson asked him what I did. He pulled up these photographs of t-shirts that I had been making—trompe l'oeil with baby owls in the pockets. We're biologically programmed to like baby animals, so I thought if I put them on a t-shirt people would want to buy the t-shirt. [*laughs*] I put different things in the pockets, sometimes animals, sometimes talismen. They had different themes. Anyway, at the time that's where I was at.

Andrew: Hudson said, "I only have one t-shirt. But I would wear *that* one." And twenty minutes later Kim walked in. I remember how impressed he was with them, and later even put them in an exhibition.

Kim: It was just a really nice chemistry and beginning.

*Kim, you shared with me some of the emails that you eventually began to send each other. It was very nice to see how your relationship grew over his last year.*

Kim: There's this one quote from our emails that I've been thinking a lot about. I'm kind of going over, like, what did I learn from Hudson? This is a non-sequitur, but around October before he died [in February] we had been talking about going through slumps, hard times. I mentioned the idea of "lifting and falling," and he really responded to it. Lifting and falling became a thread of volleyed encouragement between us. He said:

> kimkimkim, today i am lifting a lil, trying to get my smile going and feel the lite and light in me. wuda loved to return to bed and not leave the house if not the bed. gotta get out of this slump, rise and shine. yoga helps for sure, ditto meditation, work too. but i need feeling.

And I kind of feel like that might have to do with a real-time connection between art and sensuality that Hudson was able to make so naturally. Even if it's just speaking with somebody at a restaurant, or an artist, and he sees their work and is instantly really into it.

It's like, yeah, I can do all these things that balance out my nervous system in this world that feels very stressful, especially now. But I think there's this aspect of feeling and experiencing directly, not through a strict eye-to-brain agenda, but from a fully embodied ambient intelligence. It's fast, it leaves no trace. Like grace, you can only tempt its appearance. And it's not always positive or angelic. Sometimes it can be more fraught and, I don't know, funny. It's a consciousness that for me seeks sweetness and holds vast complexities. How can we make all this enjoyable despite the inevitabilities? Hudson seemed to me to walk around a lot of the time with this presence. It had the seed of this edge between living and dying. I think we found this together, or he helped to bring it out in me.

As the years have gone by since Hudson passed, I've come to understand that this is something rare for me to find in other people. It's kind of like having one foot here on the planet and one foot somewhere else. It's also something that is hard to talk about, and lends itself to stream-of-consciousness, almost like channeling weird poetry. It is an instantaneous connection. A tripped wire. It doesn't really get through the parts of the brain that are especially analytical.

This reminds me of Hudson's letter to Jonathan Hartshorn that was handed out at his memorial, where he wrote about "the opportunity to honestly experience the flattened perspective that associative thinking puts on the seriously humorous intricacies of life." Being around Hudson felt like this opportunity come true.

Here is another email bit from Hudson:

> just b n these days, whether head or hind, just b n.
> like you lotsa fallin and liftin.
> so much weight, goin on a diet.

## JUDY LINN

*Photographer*

*You were in Hilton Als' and Darryl A. Turner's 1989 show at Feature,* I Only Want You To Love Me. *Did you know Hudson at the time?*

No, I didn't know him. That was completely through Hilton and Darryl. I wasn't familiar with the gallery before then.

*Then some years later you began showing there regularly.*

I was in the 1995 Whitney Biennial—the Klaus Kertess-curated one—and after that Hudson sent me a letter in the mail asking me to be in the gallery.

No studio visit, nothing. Just "Do you want to be in the gallery?"

*What did you think?*

Wow, what a prince. Yes, of course, please. It was so lovely, like a fantasy of how things should work but never do.

*Did you have a gallery at the time?*

I had a gallery in Michigan, the Susanne Hilberry Gallery, but that was about it. I would be in group shows here and there. I was in the Diego Cortez PS1 [*New York/New Wave*, 1981] show where everyone but me began a big career. [*laughs*] But I didn't have a formal gallery in New York. I had been in 55 Mercer Street, an artist cooperative gallery. My friend Tom Nozkowski had been a member and he recommended that I join. It was really good experience. I had I don't know how many shows there, but from that experience I got rid of a lot of my pre-conceived ideas of what I wanted to do. By the end of showing there, I hated the openings, I hated the beer, I hated the pretzels, I hated my friends, I hated the whole thing. Hudson had a way of showing that was much cleaner than that.

*Did it become a close relationship?*

Well, I know other artists who tell me they talk to their dealer every day on the phone. Obviously that is a much tighter dealer relationship than I have ever had. With Hudson it was much more formal. I didn't hang out with Hudson. But showing him photographs was always really interesting. He was ready to see anything that I wanted to bring in. When we first talked, he said he wasn't interested at all in any of the Patti Smith or Mapplethorpe photographs that I was known for. And I thought, wow great, that's terrific. I was really glad about it. So he didn't actually know what photographs I had. I think he'd seen a few. But I loved that he said that they were not in the mix. But years later when those photographs were finally printed in a book, it was through Hudson.

*Do you think Feature's broad reach influenced your work?*

Yeah, I think so. In the beginning I was kind of terrified, so I fumbled around. But Hudson was terrific, very receptive. And he had shows that I loved. He had a show about Candy Darling. It was a history lesson. It was so beautiful. It wasn't about items to buy, it was an investigation into a very interesting person's life. Actually the most spectacular thing I remember, that I really loved—he did an evening presentation by a man who talked and gave the audience things to smell, aromas and perfumes [*Maison Anonyme*]. It was wonderful. He told how different cultures used aromas to tell stories and their histories. Things to smell were passed around to the seated audience. It was very intense. By the end I was completely taken over by it. I looked at the man who was seated next to me, and I said, "Can I please smell your watch?" I don't know where in me that came from. I've never asked anybody anything like that before or after. I didn't know the guy, but somehow it made sense at that moment.

And there was one show where a woman who worked with corrugated cardboard had made a beautiful, complex sculpture of a tower [*Mai Braun*]. It was in the hallway in front of the gallery before you really entered. It wasn't an extensive show by her but it was beautiful. There was another show by a woman who worked on leather. I liked that because I thought, oh yeah, leather. That's food. He did these shows, some were well-received and by well-known artists, but there were these strange other ones that I thought were fascinating. He also had artists that I just really liked, like Richard Rezac, Nancy Shaver, David Shaw, and Kinke Kooi.

*The program itself was stretchable.*

Yes, and I liked that. I didn't want to be in a gallery that just showed photographs. The photo ghetto seemed boring. It was more, "Oh, at Feature I can show a photograph next to a log." [*laughs*] Much more interesting.

*He didn't really rep photographers besides you...*

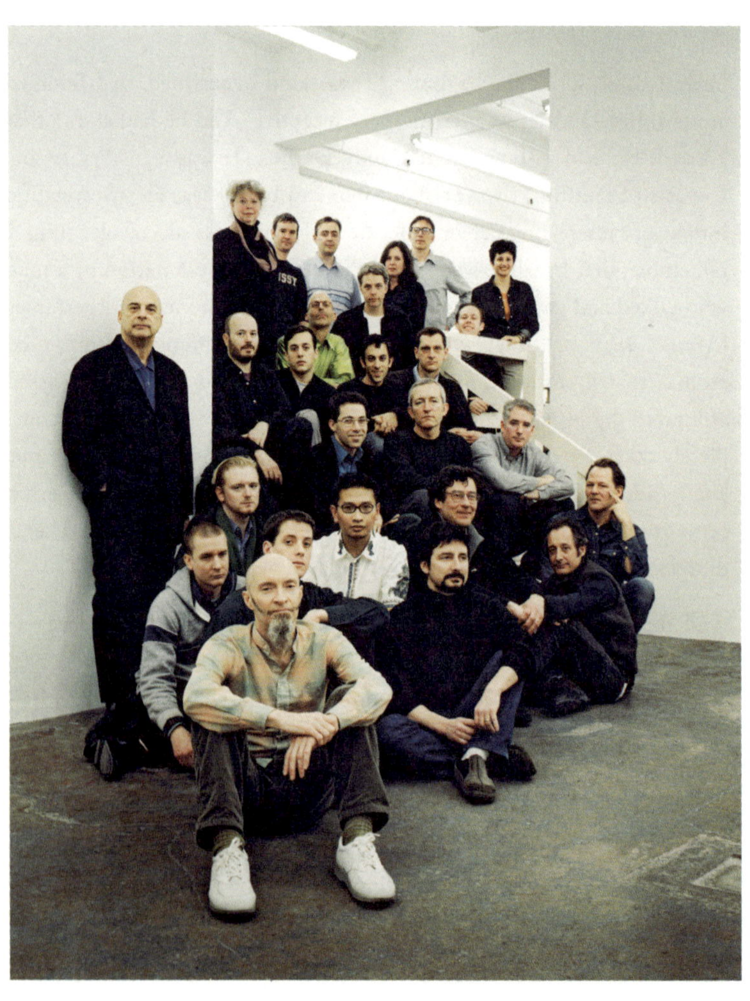

Hudson and "Feature Creatures" for *i-D* magazine, 2003. Top Row: Nancy Shaver, Jimi Dams, Jim Pedersen, Alexander Ross, Judy Linn, Richard Kern, Martin Bland, Lisa Beck. Middle row: John Torreano, Lucky DeBellevue, Sam Gordon, B. Wurtz, Alan Weiner, Michael Lazarus, Jerry Phillips, David Moreno, Jason Fox. Bottom row: Gary Batty, Jesse Bransford, Hudson, Bruce Brosnan, Lorenzo De Los Angeles, David Shaw, Richard Bloes, Dike Blair, Bill Komoski. Photo: Rainer Hosch

...and Richard Kern. Yeah, I do not want to speculate why he did not show more photography.

*What stands out to you about the gallery in its successive eras?*

I loved all the Roy McMakin furniture that he used. And I loved that at the West 25th Street gallery, the stairway to the office area, which I guess had once been a loading dock, was disconnected from the rest of the gallery. I liked that it could be moved away, which made a sort of moat separating the display area from the business area so, if needed, you could lift the drawbridge. Once when I was there, looking at photographs, or looking through something else, I realized Hudson was on the phone with an art supply store ordering chipboard. I was thinking, "Why is he doing that? Why doesn't someone else do that?" I was just kind of amazed at his willingness or maybe compulsion to do that. I mean, he had people working for him.

*What are your feelings about the business side of the gallery?*

You know, I'd sit around with other artists and they'd all complain about their dealers, and I really couldn't complain about Hudson. Of course it's a business relationship and there's going to be ups and downs. If I start nitpicking or going into things that annoyed me, things I wanted that I didn't get, or blah blah blah, it just seems like sour grapes. My career is my responsibility, it wasn't his. If he could move some product, great. But it was up to me, and I respected that. Also, I don't want to come off as too much of a complaining loser. [*laughs*] But if we had problems, he would address them. Also he did do this one amazing money thing for me. I sold some photographs through someone else, another dealer. And that dealer decided that they were not going to pay me the nice amount of money owed me. I told Hudson about this, and he said, "Okay, I'll pay you the money." I don't know what his relationship to the other person was, but Hudson bellied up the money.

*You and David Shaw had the last exhibitions at Feature.*

That show was put together on fairly short notice. Hudson called saying that something had fallen through, and he wanted to do a show of my photographs. It was a fast turnaround but it didn't actually get hung until after he was gone. But the Friday before he died I had another show opening up in Albany, and he came to that. Which means he had to take a train up to I don't know where, Hudson or someplace like that, and then take a cab across and up the Hudson River. It was a real schlep for him. And he did it. And then he died on Sunday. But on that Friday I thought, "Wow, this is great. Hudson came. I'm so amazed." It was very generous of him.

## AARON SINIFT

*Artist*

In 2004 I was just trying to get a job in a gallery. I was systematically going down West 25th Street, dropping off my resumé with every one. I remember walking into Feature, which I'd never heard of. Everyone in the galleries along the street had been ignoring me or dissing me or whatever, but here the receptionist had a quality of complete disengagement that I hadn't seen before. The gallery itself had an antiseptic quality that was more like a doctor's office. Like an experiment, in a weird way. I almost didn't leave my resumé. I thought, "This is strange. Maybe not for me." But I went ahead. I was feeling game and I needed work.

A week or two later I was in Prospect Park landscape painting and I got a phone call. The person on the other end introduced himself as the director of Feature, and said that he was interested in my resumé. Would I like to come in and meet about a potential job? I remember thinking, oh, it's that shitty gallery up towards 11th Avenue. But we talked, and he liked that I was *plein air* painting. We made an appointment and I came to the gallery two days later. I seated myself in one of those amazing Roy McMakin armchairs he had in front of his desk. Hudson had a goatee about nine inches long. I'd never seen anything like it. And he had those long slanted eyes that make you think of Siberian shamen. He was captivating in that sense, and immaculately turned out. He asked me about myself. I told him I was from Iowa, and that I'd just come back from India. He liked both of those. I had almost no experience in art handling. I didn't really know how to do anything but I was pretty upfront about it. He said that was an advantage as well, because it meant he didn't have to un-train me. He told me I was a strong candidate. So I gave him a copy of this book I'd just had printed in India. It had drawings and paintings that I'd done. "Whether or not I get this job, I'd like you to have this." That's why I'd made the book, certainly for someone like him. I left, and later he called and told me he wanted to try me out.

*What impressed you in your early days there?*

Hudson told me he preferred that people come in early and be ready to start on time. He showed me where I'd work, and I realized we'd practically be right on top of each other. No walls between us. He was showing me where I'd find all the tools, where paintings were stored, how they were arranged in racks around the room. Everything was amazingly sensible. There was not a single bit of waste in the whole place. At other galleries they want you to come in and "fix this problem." But this was a place where my job was simply to keep things at the high level that they already were.

Even in the bathroom, he explained, there were to be at least four, and no more than eight, rolls of paper towels on the shelf. On the left there should be no more than six rolls of toilet paper available, no fewer than two. [*laughs*] Throughout the gallery everything got wiped down every time anyone used it. But this attention to detail applied throughout. He told me that the preparator job was something he loved to do and would actually prefer to do himself because he knew the whole practice. He showed me exactly how to do certain things, like how to cut a box to fit just so. How to cover the edges and corners. It was a challenge, and I realized quickly that it would get boring if I didn't get into it. So I chose to rise to it and do everything to the degree expected. It was interesting, because it did make the day into kind of a game. He showed me some tricks that served me well. Little sensible things. Where you put the tab on a glassine envelope. Everyone thinks it goes this way when you pull it towards you and tape it down, when really you should do it the opposite way so that you could pull it off without tearing the glassine.

*Sounds Talmudic.*

Because it was an anticipatory science. You anticipated the complications that someone on the receiving end would have. Or anticipate the least amount of knowledge it would take them to have to re-do what you were doing. Think it through in reverse. It was for me to make it so simple and so elegant, and with as few moves as possible. It became a little bit of an obsessive game between he and I. I remember one of Steven Keister's pieces sold, a small piece about ten inches tall. Ceramic with a lot of parts sticking out. Maddeningly fragile. I made a box that you would set the piece down into, and in such a way that you could fold the sides up on it, and seal it with just two pieces of tape. It was really weird, but it was gorgeous. You could probably roll it down the stairs and the piece would still be intact.

*This was a remarked-upon aspect of the Feature "brand," if you will.*

Well, I realized that the first impression anyone had of the work that they'd purchased when it would arrive at their home would be the packaging. So what I did was a facet on the face of what Hudson was attempting to do.

The second day I was there I noticed that he would burn incense in the gallery at night. And he had these kind of brass mantra plates in different areas. Such as way above the door by the ceiling. It finally dawned on me that he was treating this as a spiritual practice. I'd just come from India, spending a fair amount of time in temples and around sadhus, and seeing how people were relating there. And Hudson was doing the same thing. It was like hanging out with a sadhu in a way. A lot of sadhus have a very fierce aspect. They're not all Candyland and hugs. They play some pretty rough games. What he was doing fit that worldview. It was our primary bond, I think. It's why we came to love each other.

*You knew assistants and preparators working at other galleries. How different was your experience from theirs?*

People were always a little bit disgruntled at other galleries. But the things that they were complaining about were not things that were my problems. For example, he was never trying to rush me. He asked me to write the labels on the packages as carefully and calmly as I could. If I was writing an address on a box, I should breathe and write clearly and carefully, so that nothing looked rushed. I realized that this was the introduction to how people would relate to the work. It underwrote the wildness of some of it, the transgressive nature, by introducing a radical level of absolute control and precision, so that nothing was undermined by any sense of unclarity. This was not as simple as creating a mystique.

In the same way, when any slides or work came into the gallery for any reason, even if it was unsolicited or wasn't at all interesting, no matter what it was, we treated it equally. It was an ethic that I wasn't seeing anywhere else. He was able to address the hierarchy within the art world through an absolute rigor that respected everyone. He never yelled at anyone. Which was also very unusual. [*laughs*]

Another thing different was that the artists always got paid first. After a show that was how he cut checks. There was a Chelsea dealer notorious for not paying artists. I know people that were showing with him, that were making a lot of money for the gallery, but who were owed tens of thousands of dollars. They were having trouble with their rent because the dealer wasn't paying them. All these different galleries had terrible reputations that way. There was an artist who was spending a huge amount of money on fabricating her work and wasn't getting paid back, even as galleries were selling it. As she was being celebrated, she was still trying to figure out how to pay for her studio. I would hear this from the assistants, and it was very, very common to hear it. That's why Hudson had such loyalty. He in turn showed his artists a level of loyalty that was rare. And I think in the end he was hurt by that.

Some people say that he pitted the workers against each other. That's not what it was. He wasn't interested in creating discord. He was interested in curating his own environment, because he spent so much time in it. But I'd been there about a year and a half, and someone I knew said to me, "You're still at Feature?" The impression that he had, and others had, was that the preparators were kind of a changing cast that kept it interesting around there. Hudson probably thought, "Oh, he'll get good at what I train him to do and then move on and take those skills somewhere else." So I did confront him about it, and we kind of had it out. I think he did want change, and liked the idea of wrapping up that chapter, and I was perceived as part of a chapter. That's only my guess. But I stayed.

Hudson had this uncanny knack of telling me all of the things he wanted done during the course of the day, but he never gave me too much and he never gave me too little. And I was almost always busy all day long. He seemed to know exactly how long everything would take. There were times I could read a book. He didn't mind, if I'd done absolutely everything I could think of. I really loved that he would respect that.

*Can you outline a criteria he had for Feature?*

He told me that if he understood it, then he wasn't interested. It was what he didn't understand that attracted him.

Another thing. I'd been there about a year or so. I'd been reading about tantra, and Hudson and I could speak together in the language of that a little bit. And I commented to him that I thought that [a certain artist] might be doing himself psychic harm through the paintings that he was making. There's something deeply transgressive and violent in this artist's work, which I think is fascinating because he's so calm on the exterior. Hudson thought perhaps, but that it was something that the artist was doing and he was doing it naturally. He just had to do it. At that moment it occurred to me that the criteria for the artists that he was showing was somehow beyond this lifetime. For me that made perfect sense, that he might be curating his gallery beyond this moment, this plane of existence even. I began seeing that a lot of the work he was showing was by outsiders that would have no chance anywhere else. He was providing a vehicle for people whose work would have gotten them arrested in some places.

*Was there a sales method?*

My dad was a siding salesman, a tin man. So I grew up around that. At Feature, I was the guy holding the art that Hudson was showing to potential buyers. But he was the softest pitch man I've ever heard. I never saw a guy put less pressure on than him. He never tried to tell anyone what was good for them, or what they wanted. He wouldn't pull out everything. He would just show a few pieces and allow them to relate to it. He wouldn't try to tell them what they were seeing. I was really moved with how he went about that. He never gave off a feeling of desperation to make a sale. It was very amiable. And that was key. "I'm here because I want to be here." No disdain. And that was part of his cultivation of reputation.

*What can you say about his relationships with other dealers?*

I knew that he was annoyed by Larry Gagosian showing up to start poaching his artists. And I know the story of how he threw [one big collector] out of the gallery. But in general I was amazed at how much positive attention he got from upper-tier dealers. This was not so much appreciated

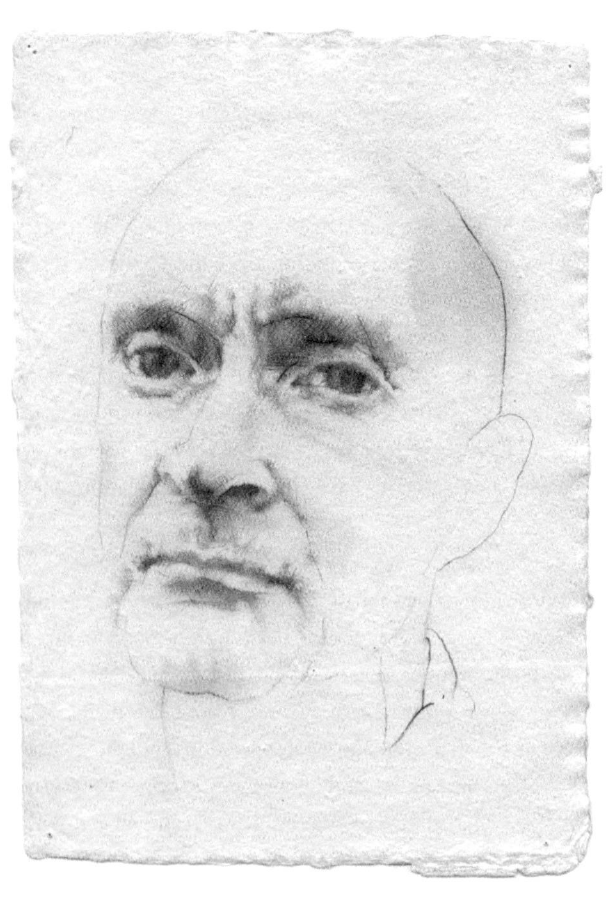

Michael St. John, *Hudson #2*, 2010. Graphite on paper, 9 x 6.5 inches

by Hudson, but you had to play with them if you wanted to be a part of that world.

*Did he?*

I think he tried to break into the upper tier of the gallery world. Around 2008, when he left West 25th Street and opened down on Bowery, that move was designed to up the game. He explicitly told me that. He was coming to the conclusion that if he wanted to hold onto artists he was going to need to provide them with more resources. Also, higher prices. He said that he would have to start selling twice as much as he had before to pay for the new gallery. That was a big switch. And I tried to make the personal choice that I was going to help him do that, as best as I could.

*He closed West 25th Street in October 2007, and then spent nearly a year on hiatus, remodeling a space on the Bowery to be the next phase of Feature Inc.*

And for all those months we didn't work, he paid us the entire time.

*That is phenomenal.*

We didn't take a pay cut at all. We offered to take one. When he was doing that whole build-out we realized, wow, he's putting himself into a lot of debt. We got $25 an hour. We did not suffer at all. We would come in, but there wasn't much art stuff to do. So we would do light construction, like sand the pillars to perfection. [*laughs*] But the remodeling turned out taking way too long, about nine months. It ended up being much more expensive to do it. Hudson was thinking more along the lines of a restorationist, because he'd signed an eleven-year lease. His thinking was, this is where I'm going to make my last stand. That's what he told me. "This is it. In eleven years I'm going to retire." But his long view didn't necessarily meet the economics of the time. As soon as the housing market went down, I knew the economy was going to collapse. By the time the thing came about there was nothing that he could do.

*He opened that space in September 2008 with a large group exhibition. And then on September 15th, Wall Street crashed. He told me that he had a full roster of appointments with collectors who were eager to get back to business with him. And then one by one they started cancelling.*

He was blindsided. It was bad. He had to start laying off people. The receptionist was the first to be laid off, because there was no need for a receptionist. And then Hudson's assistant. The rest of us said, "We'll all take a pay cut. We'll reduce our pay to whatever it is in order to keep people working." But we looked it over and did the math and decided it was probably better for us to go on unemployment. And that's what we did. I mean, it was ultimately Hudson's decision. But we were all deeply invested emotionally in his success, and nobody wanted to leave him. Nobody wanted to go. We adored him. He had been so decent to us during that whole time of the renovation.

*He was close to calling it quits after the crash. Then he saw the little space on Allen Street and made the decision to reinvent Feature on a smaller scale.*

Right around then I was offered a job working for Francesco Clemente, at his studio. But I turned it down, so that I could help Hudson move into the place on Allen Street. This was not the time to leave him.

You know, everywhere I went, if I told someone I worked at Feature, people treated me with noticeably more regard. Big galleries, little galleries. I got a lot of respect that I wouldn't get any other way. Or if it was a young ambitious artist, they wanted to know me. I mean, there was a clear reason for that. To so many, Hudson was a living legend.

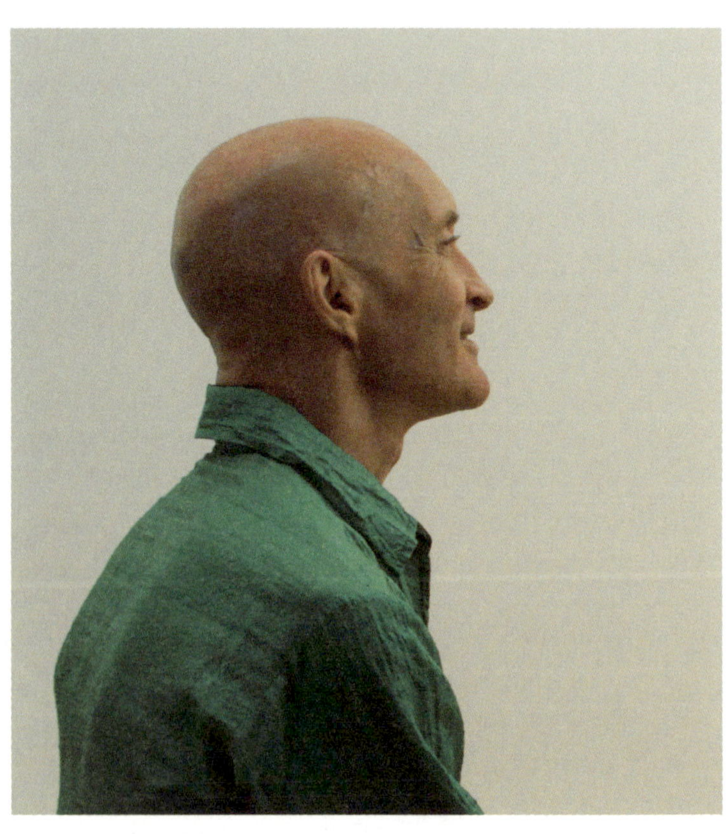

New York City, 2013. Photo: Steve Lafreniere

## HILTON ALS

*Writer and critic. Eulogy delivered at the memorial for Hudson, October 2014, Judson Church, New York City*

Hudson is dead and I cannot believe it. In the way that I can never believe time is passing when it's passed. You look up from one experience and you put your head down to another and you think days, at most months, have passed. But looking up from my desk now, I remember the first time I saw Hudson was almost twenty-five years ago. I was not yet thirty. I cannot believe it. The first time I saw him wasn't even in the gorgeous flesh, but a photograph. The picture appeared in the *Village Voice* when he moved to New York, and the article was about his pilgrimage from Chicago, a place I had never been. Where was that? I didn't know anything at all. The article went on to describe his little space on Broome Street and its distinctly political aesthetic. So many of our friends had died of AIDS. The world was such a hard, unreal place then. And I remember being at a friend's flat in the Village when I read that article in the *Voice*. And I looked at the black and white photograph of this man who went by a single name, and he was wearing a cap the way my father wore a cap, but more attractively. And I told my friend, also now dead, look at this guy Hudson's eyes. They were like the eyes of the most beautiful fish or turtle ever. "I'm going to get him to fall in love with me, and give me and Darryl a show." At the time I made big art things with my friend Darryl Turner, the photographer, but we had yet to do anything in a gallery. I wanted to make an installation and Hudson seemed so open from the article, and New York was such a different place then. I'll show you how different in a minute. I'm trying to catch my breath. I cannot believe Hudson is dead. But in any case, New York was so different then that you could write to a gallerist like Hudson a letter and they actually responded. That's what I did. I wrote Hudson a letter, and he invited me to come to his space, and I went by, and

I really did want to make him mine. He looked even better in person than he did in the photograph. And what I found even charming about him was his sense of humor and the fact that he had something wrong with his knee and he was curing that, he showed me, by taping a grain of rice to that leg. Now, I come from a family of very strange men. I'm always attracted to some version of them. And there was Hudson sitting on his little stool, with Jim nearby, and he said I could of course make an installation in his space. And Darryl and I got to work. In fact Hudson sold one figurine from the show. The tiniest thing in the show had sold for like ten dollars. It was a complete joy to him. I mean it. When I went by the gallery that day he held it up and exclaimed, eyes glistening, "One figurine, sold!" And it was the best feeling in the world for both of us. Not selling something, but saying something in the world. And to this day when I meet gay men in the art world who use their difference to push their agenda, but what they're really interested in is shopping, and in glory, and not the values that Hudson put forward, I am always disturbed, if not angry. After a while things changed between me and Hudson, and they got complicated because, oh, why go into all that right now. Messiness is the work of the stupid, living people. And I can't even believe Hudson is dead. But I loved calling him Dad. And I loved when he wrote to me. He'd sign his letters Hud Dad. And I loved him sitting on my lap at some unbearably fussy event uptown. And looking up from my desk now all I can see are his eyes and the fact that I wanted him to love me.

## NANCY SHAVER

*Artist. Eulogy delivered at the memorial for Hudson, October 2014, Judson Church, New York City*

Hudson.

Hello Nancy Shaver.

Every conversation, every correspondence began that way.

Hello Nancy Shaver.

How my name sounded, that combination of sounds, was me from Hudson. Hello Hudson. I always found his greeting comforting, both very formal and intimate.

Over the years, we had what I thought of as our five-minute meetings: about business, sometimes about art. Fourteen years of five-minute meetings.

Hello Nancy Shaver.

There was a time when I was puzzled by these extremely short exchanges, then I changed. I began to be proud of them… In five minutes we attended to business, friendship.

Feature.

Feature was in three different places in my belonging. I think it was in two others before I joined. The spaces I knew were small and peculiar. Twenty-Fifth Street had a large space, that was small, and a small space which was smaller. Hudson worked or resided on the two-step-up balcony level. There was storage to the left on the balcony, there was exhibition space for one work, and Hudson's office. Work was installed, as I remember, around his head, above his desk.

The next Feature was to be on the Bowery. The dream Feature. It was a giant raw space. When it was finished it was again about the size of his old spaces!

His office was in front, everyone in a room to the left of the door hard at work.

The large spaces were behind a door at the back of the gallery. We were hardly there. I think I was told that the space is now a shoe store.

Feature went into storage for awhile. Feature appeared again on Allen

Street. One gallery space, a medium-sized rectangle, a pleasing size. Hudson, Anne Doran, and Nathaniel Robinson working at the back of the gallery. The visitors' chairs, Roy McMakin rockers, were backed up against the raised trapdoor to the basement. B. Wurtz tumbled down the stairs and had to have stitches. I was always careful around the stairs, which began in a hole to the side of Hudson's desk.

When Hudson addressed us as a group we were Feature Family or Feature Creatures. A motley group of people making things, art works with their own hands, mostly. "Following their noses"… whatever that means. Hudson trusted us to follow our noses. We were all in a boat following our noses. A group of people making work that demanded the full attention of whatever was their particular experience. We trusted his eye. Hudson followed his nose. He created a business, of sorts, the way a painting is made, the way a sculpture comes into view.

He showed my work for fourteen years, without much remuneration. I apologized after another show without sales for being a deadbeat. He said good work didn't make deadbeats.

He worked for Feature without a break, with all his energy. Maybe Feature became his art project. He proudly kept it going against the odds, against the industry.

He was fierce.


## RICHARD KERN

*Photographer. Eulogy delivered at the memorial for Hudson, October 2014, Judson Church, New York City*

There are a lot of people here, and Hudson would appreciate that. More people than came to his openings usually.

My relationship with Hudson was a business relationship. I didn't have much of an outside relationship with him. The first thing you figured out was that Hudson had moods. There was either "Hi, glad to see you" mood, or there was busy mood. Once I figured that out, it was very easy to do business with him. The best mood was after a weekend, and he'd say, "I had the most wonderful weekend." And that meant he was at a party.

Feature was the first place I asked if I could show, the first place I went. But Hudson told me that I'd shown films at his gallery in Chicago. It was when I was a drug addict, and I didn't remember.

One of the best things about Hudson: Anyone who's in the art biz knows that you get burned all over the place. That's part of the business. But Hudson was completely honest. Nothing but honesty. That's the thing artists treasure more than anything else. I remember once I called him and said, "Hey, can I have some of that money? I have some bills to pay." I said I felt so guilty asking about this. And he said, "You shouldn't feel guilty! It's your money!" That's another thing I've never experienced anywhere else.

The first show I had there, I walked in and Hudson said, "Oh, blank was just here!" It was a big critic, for a big newspaper. I said, "Really?" And he said, "Yes! She ran right out!" He saw the look on my face and said, "Oh, don't worry. As long as your pictures are bothering people, you're doing really good." He also told me it would take people twenty years to get what I was doing. He was my advisor and the only person that I would go directly to with any question that I had. Is this a good place? Is this a good thing?

Generally Hudson didn't give a crap about money. He didn't care if you sold or not. Once I walked in and he said, "Ah, Richard. Another person that I can't sell." But he did sell occasionally.

There was a lot of time that Hudson was down, especially toward the end there when he was really, I felt, fed up with the art world. And I would talk to him about it. I said, "How can you do this? You have to go out there and pretend that you're into all this stuff, and all these people." And he would get this look on his face.

There were two times that you could always count on Hudson to be really happy. One was right when your show was first on the wall. He would walk out and say, "Ah, it's beautiful. It's beautiful." Validation right there from dad. If dad says it's good then there must be something there, even if you have your own doubts.

The other time I would see him happy was, you'd come in the gallery and he'd say, "This weekend I met the most beautiful boy. It was so incredible." What I finally understood about him was that he was such a romantic and the possibility of a romantic relationship was so important to him that the only thing in the world—and there are a lot of people like this, myself included—the only thing that came close to that feeling was the art world. It gave him the same kind of feeling, the same kind of joy. Because the art world doesn't make any sense, like relationships. It's something you stumble upon. You don't know what to expect. Sometimes something happens to you, and it's a pleasure. A small pleasure that makes the world seem, "Okay, it's not so bad."

Thanks, Hudson.

## DAVID SHAW

*Artist. Eulogy delivered at the memorial for Hudson, October 2014, Judson Church, New York City*

Hello Hudsons.
Hello Creatures.

No one story encapsulates Hudson's importance to me.
He was too important.
He was the most important person in my life.
I don't know how to say it any other way.

Besides, how do I sum up a relationship that had email exchanges that went like this:

*hello da shaw,*
*huddy af coo bd giffy 4 ya butt too big to cari by me weewee sef.*
*nex time u in da citi w the gazz guzzler lem me kno n come bi.*
*hf*

And

*ski,  crack the piece – sculpture.  outpeace h*

Just to be clear, that was a business deal.
Those were business emails.
The others were weirder and more personal.
Communication with him confounded any easy description.
The personal and the professional coalesced.

In figuring out what I was going to say tonight I didn't know where to begin. And after many false starts, I found this thing I wrote in the blackout
that was Valentine's Day 2014, just days after he died.

I don't even remember writing it.

"Don't be afraid.
Be yourself.
H."

Hudson came on like lightning.

Like a clear jolt of consciousness and mischief.

Hudson touched my sternum when I met him. He touched me with the
lightest of physical touches.
He was the lightest of physical beings.
Just one digit, extended and knowing. It was the kind of touch that bolted
right through me, and showed me how constructed I was.
Yet he was gentle and electric.

I was introduced to Hudson on the street in front of his first gallery in

SoHo, his first gallery in New York, the one that changed things here for good.  I was introduced by a friend who simply said,
"You have to meet Hudson."
As we walked down Broome Street toward 484, a sprightly elfin figure popped out of the basement below.  He was coming up dirty from packing artwork himself, I was told he did everything himself, and the cuffs of his jeans were rolled up.  So were the sleeves of the thin, sweaty t-shirt that hung low on his neck.

A giant green "Q" was printed off-center on the front of the shirt.
Two little "f"s hung in its curl.
He later told me it stood for Queer Friends of Feature.

"Fancy Wand" was writ vertically on his right, my left

and all I remember of the back
in the chaos of type and typefaces
was BUTT 2000
with what looked like a flower or an asterisk or both.

I was about to show some work at an artist-run collective in a sixth floor walk-up in Tribeca. "Give him a card," Bob said. I feigned looking through my pockets and said,
"I may have one here somewhere.
Let.
Me.
See..."
even though we had been doing this for over an hour and one was already in my hand.

Bob stifled a laugh.
Hudson just reached out, squinted softly and smiled, that smile that showed he knew everything about me before I could even look up, and said,"Ohhh, Youuuuuuu,"
and then he touched me.

Right in my center.

That was it.

Lightning.

He came to the show.
He said something about how I forced my ideas into the material.
He said he liked that.
But I really have no idea whether he thought "liking" that was a good thing.
I was hooked.
I saw a man, a real man, look and think and see through all that was before him. No pretension.
He didn't care that most of the work was shit.
He knew most work everywhere was shit.
He was always looking, always letting it in, opening up to what was around him to see if someone found something interesting, to see if someone could change his mind.
Hudson didn't care how much you knew.

He did care what you knew, because he was forever interested.

July 08, 2008
*Skier, discovering supersceedes most all.  h*

January 20, 2014
*breath n smile n forget n pay attention. friend says reticulation is the word—he said: reticulation means networking, making connections, whether its your syn-apses or with people.  interesting, yes?*

Here's a good one.
Out of the blue, October 24, 2007
All caps:

*PAY ATTENTION MOTHERFUCKER*
*ski - x - h*

We all carry in us a gift that Hudson gave us. Some fragile and

overwhelming gift he shocked into our systems.
We wouldn't be here otherwise.

Once, I sent him this with the title as the subject line:

*Animals*

*Have you forgotten what we were like then*
*when we were still first rate...*

You all know the Frank O'Hara poem?

He immediately responded:

*Ds, amused u sent this now.*
*was an animal this past weekend*
*and green and first rate.*
*speeding.*
*it was fat*
*and i had an apple in my mouth.*
*i did tricks and certainly wasnt worried.*
*i managed it all.*
*and in the next while, a worried gallery owner no longer first rate,*
*disappearing into oblivion.*
*frightened and unable to maintain.*

*such a terif writer that mr o hara is.*
*big huggie to u ds.*

Then me to him:

*untrue untrue*
*you are first rate*
*their rating system is their own*
*turn a sharp corner*
*don't want to be faster*
*be you*

*much love*

*big hug*

*see you soon like tomorrow most likely...*

*D*

I keep finding myself wanting to share things with him.

I even wanted to share the moment I found out about his death with him.

I was texting him something ridiculous about a ridiculous artist when Steve called to tell me he was gone. All Steve had to do was say my name and next thing I knew the guards of the Albertina were laying me down on this marble plinth under an over-lifesized bronze of Prince Albert on horseback, asking, "Was ist los? Was ist los?"

I sort of came to and said, "He sculpted the asshole."

I thought of how dedicated the sculptor was to get up under that tail and define the pucker.  And how so few people would ever see his dedication, and that I only saw this because Hudson died.

I wanted to tell him that.

I think Hudson would have appreciated that.

I know he would have laughed... probably at me, but he would have laughed.


## RICHARD PRINCE

*Artist. First published in* Artspace Magazine, *February 14, 2014*

First time I met Hudson. William Olander invited me over to his place in the 20s off of Park Avenue South in December '85. Bill was or would become a curator at the New Museum when they were on West Broadway. Up till then he was a curator out at Oberlin College and had put together shows in the early 1980s with people like me and David Salle and Cindy Sherman. When I went over to Bill's apartment, the only other person there was Hudson.

Here's the thing. The moment I entered the apartment I started to have an anxiety attack and started to freak out like I was on a bummer acid trip. As soon as I entered the apartment I turned around and left. I never talked to Hudson about this "first" encounter. That was the thing about Hudson. He played it as it laid. He didn't need to know or care about your fuckups. He was interested in the art you were making.

After leaving the apartment... the next morning I got on a plane and moved to Venice Beach in California. I rented a house with some music friends and started to make drawings of cartoons. Redrawing cartoons of my favorite cartoonists. Two things happened while I was in Venice. Hudson asked me to send some of these "cartoons" to him. He said he was going to open up a gallery/performance space in Chicago.

He also convinced me to apply for an NEA. I had never applied for any kind of grant. It seemed, I don't know... a waste of time. He actually made out the forms and wrote most of the proposal. The next thing I know I got $15,000 in the mail. That was kind of like getting a million bucks in that TV program *The Millionaire*.

Never having any money was something I was used to. This was a whole new ballgame. The drawings of cartoons were done with a no. 6 soft lead pencil on hot press d'arche paper... 26-by-40. They were faithfully redrawn right down to the caption. I called them "jokes." I sent them along to Hudson and I swear the next thing I know I get a check in the mail for $3,500! Every time he sold a drawing I'd get a check. It was like finding a lost wallet. The first thing I did with the cash was get the daily newspapers delivered right to my lawn.

It's January 1986. You have to understand, this is the first time in my life I'm flush. I kept asking myself... who is this guy? And the only answer I could come up with... was Angel.

I realized that calling the cartoons "jokes" was wrong. They were cartoons. If I wanted to call them "jokes" then I'd have to get rid of the illustrative image part and concentrate on the punch line. So that's what I did. I'd moved back to NYC in early spring and started to hand-write one-liners on 11-by-14 pieces of paper. Hudson said he had finally found a space for a gallery and wanted to know if I would have the first show.

Of course. For you? Anything. Whatever you need.

That was my relationship with Hudson. There was never any hesitation. I trusted him. He created a situation for an artist like myself that I felt completely comfortable in. AND... it's where I wanted to be.

Hudson was an artist who opened a gallery. He didn't wait for permission. He didn't ask to be part of a committee or be on a board or be part of a group that would sit around and hash things out and come up with a plan. As far as I know Hudson didn't have any plans. He wanted to do what he felt and what he thought was right.

The first thing that Hudson felt right about was to show my new "jokes." I remember he sent out a mustard-colored postcard with the word JOKES printed in Helvetica bold in the middle of the card. So that was it. That's what got it started. Hudson was the first one for me.


## ANN BOBCO

*Friend. Eulogy delivered at the memorial for Hudson, October 2014, Judson Church, New York City*

Hey, Hudson…

I just have a few more questions—and THEN you can go—OK?

———————————

Do you remember when we met?
I bet you do.
You were always good at pulling out a detail from some long-ago event.

1987.
February.

It was BITTER cold.
Chicago cold…

You were bright, shiny and new to me.
You'd offered Bill (known to YOU as B. Wurtz) support and visibility in the
city of my father's birth—so I'd figured: "What's not to like?"
FEATURE felt fresh to me with its segmented areas for display.
Kay Rosen's paintings were just around the wall from B.'s new work.
It was thrilling.

LOOK at you in this photo. You, in a green, button-down shirt…!

Standing in front of that red panel I see you as both complementary AND
counterpoint to Jamie Reid's Sex Pistols graphics.
Jamie Reid on a wall of blood.
Kay Rosen and B. Wurtz on walls of ice.
What a combination for a February exhibition.

Your shirts and exhibitions almost never let me down.

———————————

Your anti-authoritarian idealism reeled me in and I was hooked for many,
many years.

From the beginning I wanted to hear how you'd become the YOU you
seemed to be.

But the YOU-you-seemed-to-be-to-me kept shape-shifting.

Do you remember the dinner we had on Suffolk Street in '89? You and Bill
were going on about The Smiths' music and Morrissey's stated celibacy.
You, too, were celibate, you said. You enjoyed extremes… Mona Lisa had
nothing on you right then, with your face so composed. Without a waste of
breath you said, "But you know, I always lie."

You were a Performance Artist with a capital "P".
From a very early age, I think…

———————————

But I digress.

———————————

Can you tell me a little more about your grandma? Your LITHUANIAN grandma? (I always loved that you and I each had one. Not that they were anything alike.) Was she the one that brought you to New York on the train? To the City that was NOT like your house? To walk through museums filled with high-ceilinged rooms? Rooms packed-with-objects-and-paintings? The City where you glimpsed the possibility of hiding in plain sight?—I just want to see a photo of you with her.

———————————

And what about your paper route? How old were you when you had it? Were you really SUCH a scrupulous saver that your entire family used you as a banker, asking for loans periodically? But money wasn't EVER your end goal. The challenge of figuring out how to construct an existence was. And working hard helped you until the end, even though it started to bring you down.

———————————

Were you at heart a Serious Kid or a Misbehavin' Boy? A mutt birthed of the two?

You were definitely a jokester.
Opening FEATURE on April 1st in 1984???
Orwell would have approved.

My take is that you aspired to sainthood… while stalking Satan. I sensed your Catholicism as a gentle bellows, pushing air slowly and steadily onto the flames of your imaginative capacity. The flames lunging upward in spasmodic jerks. I bet you went through convoluted lengths of corridors to keep the fire doors shut. To keep them tight. But the juices were boiling and flowing and could not so simply be contained.

You were too smart for the hypocrisy of The Church. But you loved the rituals and you adored the sensuality of it all. The Frankincense, the draping velvet of the Chasubles and the stiff, starched linen of the Surplices.

You were an ascetic and a voluptuary. But you weren't all about extremes—there was a deep yearning to connect to other people. Your ability to read each person you encountered and respond like the best of thermostats made many of us wonder if you came from aristocracy. No… but you were the cream of the working-class crop.

Hudson, do you remember what you said to me that October morning at St. Vincent's? It was October of '03. You were crying. You seemed hurt, too tired to be angry. SO worn down by the drugs they were giving you. You said you couldn't believe how much you'd given away.

You kept saying, "And for what? FOR WHAT?"

For us, Hudson.

## GARY INDIANA

*Writer and critic. First published in* Artspace Magazine, *February 14, 2014*

I met Hudson in 1987 or '88 in Chicago, when I was doing a book tour for my first novel—I believe he had not yet opened Feature, and was working at the Randolph Street Gallery. I found him immediately sympatico and fascinating—a lovely personality with a wonderful mind and instinctive good taste, but discerning in an intellectual way. He wasn't an Art Person whose range of interests was at all limited to Art, thank god.

I think the first or second time I saw him we went with David Sedaris, Steve Lafreniere, John Sanchez, and Ferd Eggan to a leather bar that had a back patio, where we smoked a lot of weed and snorted poppers while "ironically" watching one leather lady lick another's boots. He was really making love to those boots with his tongue, and his Master was in seventh heaven.

I had the impression that Hudson was never especially surprised by anything. He reminded me of John Waters: not judgmental when it wasn't necessary, and curious about anything people do that's out of the ordinary. I'm not saying licking boots is so arcane, but it could have been something far more extreme and I don't think either of us would have blinked.

For a few years, I was often in Chicago and I always looked him up. He introduced me to Kay Rosen and several other artists whose work became important to me.

Hudson moved to New York at a time when I had finished what I considered a disastrous longeur of writing as an art critic in the *Village Voice*. I hated that job and was intensely alienated from anything to do with the art world when I finally quit, but Feature was one of three or four galleries I could go to later without vomiting. He showed Richard Prince and Dike Blair and Candy Darling, and a lot of other people whose work meant something to me. A few months ago we talked for a long time on the phone and made the usual New York promise to see each other soon. Perhaps we will, but not here, alas. A terrible loss of a beautiful person.

## MIKE McGONIGAL

*Writer, critic and editor. Memorial essay, 2022*

For decades I have tried to explain what was so special about Feature Inc. Why was it the best gallery I have ever visited, by magnitudes? The walls were just as white as anywhere else, and I didn't always like what was in there. And just to try to relate who Hudson was? How he seemed at times like a trickster god stepped out of the background of a Jack Smith film, just hanging out for a while here, to fuck with all of our heads.

It's easy to start with the usual rattled-off list of people he showed—if not exactly first, then close enough. And if they weren't artists who later left for galleries who could advance more money and help them land in big collections and on the covers of magazines, you can drop in the list of those he continued to show despite market indifference at the time. Both lists are remarkable.

Hudson was just so beautiful. And I always wanted to say something funny, to make him laugh. It often happened when I wasn't trying too hard, which took me off guard a bit. But to feel like you personally helped keep him aloft was so great. We were friendly, though I didn't know him outside of the gallery, but he was so generous, especially when work he showed had obviously confused me. "Don't worry; just come back and look at it again," he said more than once.

And from the mid-1980s to the early 1990s when I lived in the area, I would drop by Feature as close to weekly as I could; it wasn't far from my friend Kramer's recording studio, and Kramer always had great new music and the best hash. And I was just this dumbass with a fanzine [sometimes] going to NYU. I couldn't believe my luck—that these people would share these treasures with me.

So I dropped by and I was generally high. But I didn't need to be in order to feel simultaneously awkward and in awe—but also accepted there. It's where I encountered joyous banter at its highest. I so wish I had had the presence of mind to make fly-on-the-wall recordings. Jimi, Jim, and Hudson spoke a language I barely understood, in multiple ways. And then Hilton Als would drop by and it was all I could do to catch one third of the references tossed through the air. But I knew that it was was important and insanely fun, too. It was the '90s but they weren't too cruelly ironic; I don't think they would have so warmly welcomed my ex-roommate Verity Wilcox during the Broome Street years if that was the vibe.

Hudson wrote so well about the work he showed that it's obvious he was thinking about it constantly. Like here, from a Lisa Beck show in June 2009: "for the twenty something years i have known lisa beck, the migration of the circle or sphere from one realm of meaning into another has been at the heart of her investigation. thru her use of simple formal devices including repetition, size, and spatial relationships, she creates an exchange between the visible and the invisible that saturates this elemental shape or form with resonance and duration."

Before I left Portland, Oregon a decade ago, I put on a group show with some of my favorite (mostly living) artists at a gallery in the basement of my friend's record store. I was amazed when we were able to include an elaborate Joe Brainard work sent by Tibor de Nagy, a big Bruce Conner piece thanks to a collector in New York, and three works by Feature Inc. artists (one by Kinke Kooi and two by David Moreno). That friend's store has a motto hanging over its mantle, "Love Over Gold." Maybe that could work for Feature Inc. as well?

It would have been more expensive at the time to properly ship the works back with adequate insurance, so at the start of July 2013, I bubble-wrapped them up and carried them all with me on a JetBlue flight instead. (That probably isn't art-kosher so please don't tell anyone.) The great artist and editor Billy Miller met up with me as I gratefully returned the Feature Inc. pieces. Miller remarked that Hudson seemed to give me so much attention. And I didn't know what to make of that. It sounded just a little bit jealous, but was said as a compliment.

It hit me later, thinking half-a-year later so much about Hudson upon his death, that we all were in love with and in awe of Hudson. I knew that when I last saw him I had told him that I love him, and am glad to have said those words out loud. And in the obits and in communications with friends, I realized I had known so little about his own early art career and works. And these little things, like I had known his full name but forgotten it because he was just Hudson. Why hold on to such trivia.

I think about him all the time; we all do. I remember almost daily how Hudson told me he never listened to the news or read a newspaper, and it doesn't matter if that's "true" or not. It definitely makes me wonder why I do. On the surface, all he seemed to do was to run a gallery. But in practice, he was trying to help us to see the world in actually new ways, however subtle. And he was simply trying to share joy in a world that often is so devoid of it. I'm sorry to end on such bald sentiments, but that's what I get from Hudson, this person who cared so much for others' work and who lived for—well, I'll just call it beauty, above all else.

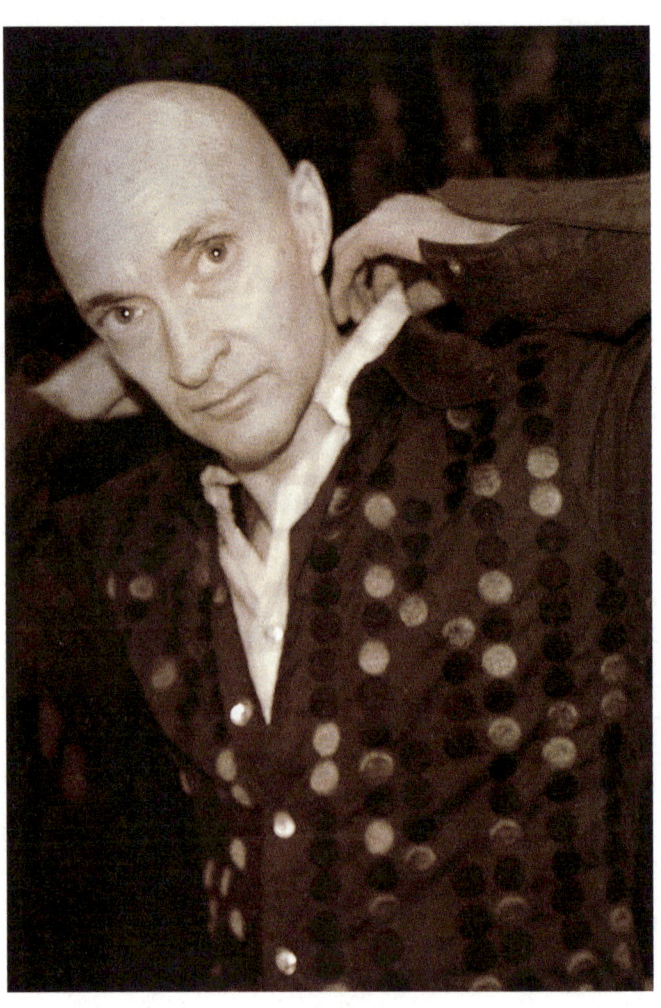

Photo: Judy Linn, 2005

# AN INTERVIEW WITH HUDSON

## DIKE BLAIR

Dike Blair: *What exhibitions are you looking forward to?*

Hudson: *Recent Autodidact*s. *Oh don't be an asshole, silly; it's just a circle. The East Village and the YBA.* Some women artists of the last twenty-five years, however not those who have been most celebrated, with essays and interviews which focus on differences between male and female art-making and art. An exhibition of noted artists' works considered to be failures or atypical. And two small, amusing exhibitions: Richard Prince re-photographs and Alex Katz paintings 1979-1988, as well, paired abstractions by Gerhard Richter and Howard Hodgkin. All up in that Imaginary Museum in my mind.

*What do you think about what museums are doing these days?*

They need to flee from hipness and the current notion of art as fun, and ditto for artists, galleries, and collectors. Museums are the big news these days, as their actions and changes deeply shape the art world. There should be a critical examination of such things as their reorientation toward mass entertainment and the scale of huge, and the expanding power of their education departments and their pervasive audio tours, which seem to churn out like-minded fact-followers rather than observant eyes. Whatever happened to the museum as a place of study, aesthetics, and the subjective, or the quiet time wandering about a museum deep in thought or ecstatic with emotion? Perhaps museums should institute one silent day weekly. Also, why are museums collecting works by artists who have had fewer than three or four one-person exhibitions? And finally, curatorial positions should be created for those with training outside academia.

*Speaking of academia, do you have any advice for the art student?*

Hand-in-hand with the museum issue is the art school: the making of professional artists who are busy with positioning themselves in careers. These years, it's probably better to develop out of art school. It's quite odd now that art-school graduates expect immediate affiliation with a gallery, believing they are already artists of some development. Generally, it requires five or so post-graduation years to disengage from the teacher/ school influences and create one's own effort. At this point I've stopped attending graduate and undergraduate art school exhibitions as a way to remain in touch with younger artists and art. I'm looking outside the box.

*It seems we could all use some of that.*

Exactly. There are many ways to get outside the current commodification of art. For collectors, I'd say, turn your back on the obvious, and favor collecting art as a passion, a curiosity, or for discovery. I even think that collecting art as decoration seems more interesting than as investment. Investment collecting is seriously changing art in a bad way. Critics could be less agenda-oriented, and artists more severe with their editing and more honest with their selection of style and subject matter. Galleries should avoid art made for easy consumption. We should all pay less attention to the salesmanship and showmanship of auctions and fairs, and, of course, be more aware of the not new or hot. And lastly, stop running around trying to see everything everywhere, and spend more time with the richness that is close to home.

*It's always struck me that you show work that runs somewhat counter to what's on view in other commercial galleries. Is this conscious, and if so, can you describe how you bounce off the status quo?*

The exhibitions at Feature are not intentionally organized to counter something. They develop out of what I am most attracted to, and my decisions are far more intuitive than intellectual. On some level I see most of Feature's exhibitions as participating in the current trends, although from a personal or oblique perspective. Generally, I prefer art that is complex and multi-focused. Such work is, and probably always has been, out there, yet because it isn't an easy read, or easy to explain, it rarely functions in the market in a very big way.

I once overheard two critics chatting about an artist, and the more noted critic mentioned that he loved the work being discussed, yet he would not write about it, as he found it too difficult to explain! To me, that seems all the more reason to write about it, or in my case, to exhibit the work.

*Usually your selections and exhibition groupings anticipate or make more concrete certain concepts that artists are reaching for. Does the sense of trend interest you at all?*

It is the artists who lead the way. Watch what they are doing and you will see what is happening. Trends do intrigue me, yet because of my hands-on approach, I usually assimilate or reject trends quite some time before they become pervasive. These years trends are so swiftly advertised and assimilated that it seems obvious to stick to one's own guns. For me, a glut of anything diminishes its power, and when that occurs, the desire for something else itches. Different people reach their saturation point at different times. Also, much depends on what understanding—art hysterical, social, and other—one brings to the evaluation. And sometimes oversaturation, the stay-and-play syndrome, may lead to something most unexpected and interesting. The process is not cut-and-dried. If one has a gallery committed to trends and sales, then surely following the cresting trend is most important. Should one have a personal gallery, one based on the owner or director's vision and ideals, or even a specific commitment to art and artists, then one follows some thread or intuition regarding the matter of when to grasp and when to let go.

*So Feature is a personal gallery, and your selections are primarily intuitive. Do you ever fear that your intuition could be reactionary?*

Definitely. For example, my current moratorium on photography, especially art-directed snapshot-quality images of low life, especially when class, gender, and sexuality are pictured. And I very much avoid the current notion of the largest possible photographs, particularly when laminated to Plexiglas. I remember traveling through the MoMA's Gursky exhibition thinking that this guy makes great postcard images and that many of them actually would be more significant at that scale and in that form. Yet if an artist presented me with photographs, or even large photographs laminated to Plexiglas, that riveted my attention, my current position would go down the drain. Even when deep in a saturated trend, there is always room for something extraordinary and more defining.

While I do make intuitive decisions regarding my selection of artists, remember that I cart around undergraduate and graduate art training, a MFA in painting, and ten years of performing as a dancer and performance artist, and I have viewed thousands of studios and slide packets. I have twenty years of visiting at least fifty or so galleries per month in the capacity of a gallery owner, and my ten years prior to Feature were spent as an administrator and curator in the not-for-profit sector.

I love what art does and we grok it in our hearts and minds. Aesthetic and socio-political decisions are more interesting to me than business decisions.

*In the early '80s you were the director of Randolph Street Gallery in Chicago. How did you come to that? How did that shape your philosophy?*

The director of the gallery headhunted me to develop a performance, live events, film, video, and music program. At the time, late '70s early '80s, I was president of C.A.G.E. That organization's curatorial and administrative approach at the time is fixed in my mind as an extraordinary model for the administration of not-for-profit, artist-oriented arts organizations—very socially unencumbered, free, direct, accessible, and responsive.

Also at that time, I had begun my administrative involvement with NAAO, the National Association of Artists Organizations, which provided me with a national overview of artists' organizations and their programs.

The '70s and '80s not-for-profit sector partially developed out of the closed system of the existing commercial galleries and its lack of reaction to the new, expanding artist communities. That helped create the format whereby an organization generally worked with an artist once, or perhaps a few times over many years. After shuffling too many artists through my programs, I realized that a lessening in my standards was endemic to the constant search for the new. (One can see how this format could encourage the development of art as entertainment.) The high turnover also made it difficult to foster the development of certain ideas or aesthetics, which seemed more important to me than a diverse, constantly changing program. So I became interested in working with fewer artists over a longer period of time, and the commercial gallery format seemed a way to economically support my thoughts.

*So I imagine that's why Feature came about? When was that?*

Feature opened on April Fools' Day in 1984, with an exhibition of Richard Prince rephotographs. The gallery name was chosen as a way to deflect a personality from the gallery, an attempt to let the exhibitions be the focus. And the structure of having several galleries simultaneously show differing exhibitions was my move against stardom and a push for pluralism and multiplicity.

*Your reputation is as an artist-friendly gallery. Your practice of looking at artists' slides and responding with a written note is legendary. How, when, and why did you start doing this?*

Sometimes those notes, which I've written since day one, cause a backlash. The most oppressive response yet, and it truly shook me, questioning my making any comment at all, was "So who the fuck do you think you are—God?"

Artists put their ego, and then some, on the line when they solicit a gallery for representation. It's an embarrassing if not demeaning process, and it's even worse if the gallery being approached is one of the artist's favorites. My concern has been to look at the work in terms of my interests and its possibility for exhibition at Feature, and ever so briefly and candidly respond to its form and content, execution, and its potential to evolve. With some frequency I request an update in a year or so. One artist presented me with work for nine years and each year it was closer and more ready, and then finally—shit happens. Now he is affiliated with Feature and having a visible success.

*How do the sheer number and intensity of these exchanges not overwhelm you?*

The lack of a wall between my office and the gallery's exhibition space is a joy but also a problem that I've not been able to resolve. So far my best solution has been to partially obstruct the entrance to the office area with a bookcase. The back of the bookcase, which faces the exhibition space, is an inoperable door. This hints at privacy while allowing for easy access to the office and the storage space behind the office. Yet it hasn't at all worked well in creating much privacy. Visitors are frequently interrupting my work with mundane questions, or unaffiliated artists' needs drive them to introduce themselves, something I find annoying as I am almost always quite obviously working. If I were leisurely sitting around, all that would be quite different. The artists who intrude don't seem to ask themselves why I would care to meet them while knowing nothing of their work. I usually attempt to disarm the intensity of the situation with a bit of friendliness and an off-the-cuff remark.

While I am at Feature I dive into the thick of things. By the end of the day I require alone time. Rarely do I socialize in the evenings following the closing of the gallery, and when I am home I maintain near silence until I return to Feature the following day. No newspapers, magazines, TV, radio, phone, video—however, sometimes music, and always cooking delicious meals.

*Do you ever consider altering or suspending your slide viewing practice?*

No, reviewing slides is important to me. I do learn many things about art and artists from the experience. And I just could not send back a package without some kind of acknowledgement, as that seems too cold, too corporate. This current, impersonal corporate model, with the invisibility of gallery staff other than a receptionist, which continues to dominate our field, is not for me. Mom-and-pop operations charm me as a form, but that doesn't mean that I do not appreciate organization and exactness.

*Speaking of modest operations, I think that the artists you work with, almost across the board, make or fabricate their own stuff. Does that sound correct? Is this simply a matter of your taste or is there a politic involved, or both?*

That's correct, but it developed over time and without deliberation. My experience has been that most artists' work cannot withstand out-of-house production. Essential things, the things that let an object live, that make it art, become lost. There are few instances when the artist's intent is so transparent to the produced objects that out-of-house production works. Usually a sense of hand allows the eye and mind to more readily linger and engage in the object and its resonance. The viewer is also vaguely reminded that a person is involved. Most outsourced production results in more attention to the surface; the object becomes a shell, and the read of that shell or surface is fast. I am more interested in the idea of being arrested by the object. The qualities brought about by the out-of-house production most often re-represent and deflate both content and meaning. Yet, again, there is room for everything, and certainly inherent to art making is an attitude that one may successfully do what was not possible before. That is a laudable and worthy attitude, one that contemporary art currently depends on.

*Do you think Chelsea gallery architecture has impacted the art?*

Well, I wouldn't exactly call it architecture.

Again, in scale, administrative layout, and personality—the suits—we see business at work, the corporate model, which I don't find rewarding or wish to encourage. Distantly related, and interesting to me, is the manner in which the galleries, perhaps due to the overabundance of concrete floors, seem to have become an extension of the sidewalk, almost as if there were no door. And so we have a further breakdown of public and private. Casual strollers, rollerbladers, carriage pushers, cell phone talkers, shoppers, lunchers, et al. move in and out of the galleries, traveling at a near consistent speed. While the democracy of that seems a good thing, somehow the art and the possibility for involvement with art suffer. With that type of situation, how may one have much of an internal experience, though there is more and more art that doesn't want or need that manner of experience? Generally, exhibitions at Feature are about interior experiences, and for some time, to encourage that sensibility, I've been contemplating installing parquet floors in the gallery. There would be an anteroom for shoes, bags, carriages, packages, etc., felt slippers for all, and relative quietness, of course, and only five or six people would be allowed in the gallery at a time. All that is scary, as it reeks of the genteel privacy against which so many have rebelled, myself included. Yet it seems right for the time, especially as it is not the dominant mode.

*Feature really caught my attention in the early '90s, when you showed at least some erotic art. This was a time when political correctness had fused with identity art, but you allowed for pleasure. Can you describe what you were responding to and creating at that time?*

Political correctness is a bad thing. It's shortsighted and encourages repression and polar reaction, rather like Shakespeare's lady: she doth protest too much. For me, art is about the mind, and the mind is an arena in which anything goes. One learns there to distinguish between the personal and the public. Morals develop as one moves through all the possibilities. Discernment is a must.

I am proud of having presented late-'80s and early '90s exhibitions of rather extreme sexual work, and especially the numerous exhibitions of the drawings of Tom of Finland. He remains a master draftsman and a major influence on so many minds and bodies and artists. Inserting his work into the discussion put the hidden agenda of the repressive politically correct, which then glutted the galleries, on the table. It's sad that Tom of Finland drawings should remain outside of art. Even to this day the dominant art worlds, especially the American versions, remain so afraid of the representation of sexuality.

During one Tom of Finland exhibition, when Feature was on Broome Street, a busload of people visited the gallery next door and a few wandered into Feature. A woman, say in her sixties, came in, carefully looked around, left, and soon returned with a male/female couple of a similar age. They were in the gallery for quite some time. On their way out, as they passed by the office, they were quietly speaking among themselves, and the woman from the couple mentioned that she thought she had just seen pornography, and the other woman replied, "Yes, but did you see the way they were drawn?" Overhearing that left me floating.

*Many consider your spaces eccentric.*

Part of that, I think, comes from the fact that Feature presents multiple exhibitions simultaneously. The current Feature uses its tiny mezzanine space as a discrete exhibition area, and we have an inoperable door space on West 20th Street known as "The Wrong Gallery." There are so many interesting artists whose work should be seen and injected into our art discussions and art markets that no space should be left unused. It is the responsibility of the galleries to challenge and broaden the market, not to acquiesce to it. One goes to art for expansion, striving, and perhaps for some experience of an Other. I'm rather opposed to art being made or presented to further satisfy more of the same.

Recently I heard a rumor that a collective of the larger contemporary art museums was considering commissioning artists to create large works, which would then tour all their spaces. You can see the dollars and careers at work luring the artists to produce works that fit within the content restrictions and scale opportunities of the museums. Given that so much is at stake, you can be assured that such a program will provide us with yet more products of fine entertainment—or is it fine products of entertainment? Art is such a fragile thing, so easily perverted, and in the long term, commissioned works are generally lesser works.

But to get back to the spaces: I believe your observation comments on the lack of experience we have with making or appreciating personal spaces, or spaces or buildings that are designed for a more particular system or idea. This is again what I see as a reflection of the dominance of sameness, the corporate mentality. All of Feature's exhibition spaces have been quite normal, if not conservative: floors, walls, ceiling, and lighting in the usual places and of typical materials. The furnishings however, are more personal and fanciful. I enjoy that in my office and my home. I am always finding more effective and interesting ways to enjoy space and furniture, and if I had my way and the time, I'd continually be renovating my home and gallery.

*I've never really known your spiritual beliefs, but I think you meditate, and you might be Buddhist? And I've always sensed that you're attracted to an art of the mind and to alternate realities. What are your thoughts about reality?*

I don't follow any specific ideology or religious belief, and I'm not a Buddhist, although I wish I had a better understanding of Buddhism. And while I have strong spiritual interests, I also keep at least one foot in the carnal garage. For about thirty years I have happily engaged in a form of contemporary, secular meditation, one that requires neither a master/ student relationship nor any need to be part of a community, yet I also wander alertly around, sampling a bit from here and there. I consider making and appreciating art a spiritual endeavor. It is generally about bringing life to some otherwise inert thing.

As for the use of the mind, well, I don't much see how not to use it when engaging with art. Not that it is the only cognitive factor involved. Internal dialogue deeply interests me.

The notion of alternate realities goes hand in hand with that. It seems to me that the world is faceted into and/or out of many realities. An examination of one's cross-cultural experiences or drug experiences sophomorically begins to expose such things, and the power of the belief in a single reality then begins to fall away. Yet I am too scientifically uninformed and experientially limited to venture any evaluation of the fullness of life. My lack of comprehension of the probable pebble of what we/I believe to be the human experience is humbling. Yet I do rather like keeping it all vague-ish, ever changing, and adaptable.

*In closing, and very generally, what has your experience as a gallerist taught you?*

One of the great things about aging and having the gallery for twenty years is that the cycles by which things come and go and return yet again become humorously obvious. The notion of the new appears in a more realistic perspective than we are generally willing to acknowledge, one involved with novelty, fashion, and style. As a result, art with deeper levels of personal meaningfulness have become increasingly important. In terms of artists, those with sincere, personal investigations hold greater magnitude, regardless of much else. It's all very freeing to be rid of this new thing, and as the urgency for mapping or recording this immediate moment decreases, a much larger world is open to appreciation.

*And if you weren't a gallerist, what might you be doing?*

Chef for a tiny restaurant. Gardener. Sanskrit scholar.

*—Dike Blair, artist*

*This interview was conducted in 2003-04. It was originally intended for* Artforum, *but was published instead in Dike Blair's 2007 book,* Again: Selected Interviews and Essays (*WhiteWalls*).

# Feature Inc.

1984-1988
340 West Huron Street
Chicago IL

1988-1993
484 Broome Street
New York NY

1993-1999
76 Greene Street
New York NY

1999-2007
530 West 25th Street
New York NY

2008-2009
276 Bowery
New York NY

2009-2014
131 Allen Street
New York NY

Avi Adler
Shinichiro Akasaka
Stephen Aljian
(Art)n
Richard Artschwager
Bill Ashley
Donald Baechler
Michael Banicki
Bastille
Gary Batty
Lisa Beck
Nancy Becker
Naomi Ben-Shahar
Matthew Benedict
Ben Berlow
Cindy Bernard
Mel Bernstine
Huma Bhabha
Ginny Bishton
Dike Blair
Richard Bloes
Lyn Blumenthal
Jennifer Bolande
Bome
Krimmer Brams
Jesse Bransford
Mai Braun
James Brinsfield
Bruce Brosnan
Alex Brown

Jared Buckhiester
Chris Burden
Kathe Burkhart
Kimberly Burleigh
Werner Büttner
Michael Peter Cain
Janet Carkeek
Lance Carlson
Sarah Charlesworth
Jack Carter
Joe Cavallaro
Todd Chilton
Nancy Chunn
Larry Clark
Bruce Clearfield
Janet Cooling
John Coplans
Josh Criscione
Carl D'Alvia
Hanne Darboven
Lorenzo De Los Angeles
Lucky DeBellevue
Michael and Sharon Demcsak
David Deutsch
Steve DiBenedetto
Stephen Dillemuth
Eric Doctors
John Dunn
Jean Dunning
Gabriele Dziuba
Bill Emrich
Robert Engel
Kate Ericson
Dustin Ericksen
Fred Escher
Bruno Fazzolari
Vincent Fecteau
Jeri Felix
Arnold Fern
Carl J. Ferrero
Julia Fish
Kip Fitzgerald
Robert Flack
Bob Flanagan
Robert Fontanelli
Eve Fowler
Jason Fox
Tom Friedman
Mark Fry
General Idea
Matthew Geller
Gilbert & George
John Glascock
Robert Gober

Bill Goffrier
Pamela Golden
Mark Gonzales
Félix González-Torres
Lee Gordon
Sam Gordon
Gregory Green
Tony Greene
Alex Grey
Sue Gurnee
Léonie Guyer
Kara Hammond
Chris Hammerlein
Donna Hapac
Carol Harmel
Rachel Harrison
Joshua Hart
Jonathan Hartshorn
Richard Hawkins
Doug Henders
Arturo Herrera
Daniel Hesidence
Thrush Holmes
Mamie Holst
Jenny Holzer
Linda Horn
George Horner
Cannon Hudson
Scott Hug
David Humphrey
Peter Huttinger
Ildebrando
Tyler Ingolia
Jim Isermann
Franck André Jamme
Bill Jenkins
Howard Johnson
Larry Johnson
Ernest Jolicoeur
G.B. Jones
Clint Jukkala
Vivian Kahra
Rusty Kane
Kanishka's of Calcutta
Mike Kelley
Richard Kern
Isabella Kirkland
Selena Kimball
Jochen Klein
Sheila Klein
Todd Knopke
Douglas Kolk
Bill Komoski
Kinke Kooie

Jeff Koons
Lahangi Korwa
Joseph Kosuth
Mark Kroening
Otto Künzli
Justin Ladda
Kevin Larmon
Louise Lawler
Michael Lazarus
Judy Ledgerwood
John Lekay
Sheree Levin
Sherrie Levine
Miranda Lichtenstein
John Lindell
Peter Levinson
Judy Linn
Joan Logue
Stephen Long
Michelle Lopez
Lovett/Codagnone
Ken Lum
Mette Madsen
Gina Magid
Kevin Maginnis
Monica Majoli
Vicki Mansoor
Robert Mapplethorpe
Christian Marclay
Ralph Marsault
Martin/Holland
Chris Martin
Bruno Martinazzi
John McCafferty
Steve McCall
Roy McMakin
Allan McCollum
Jason McKechnie
Josephine Meckseper
Douglas Mellini
Scott Miller
Tracy Miller
Travis Molkenbur
David Moreno
Richard Morrison
Lillian Mulero
Heino Muller
Takashi Murakami
Catherine Murphy
Naoto Nakagawa
Darinka Novitovic Chase
Bobbie Oliver
Jeff Ono
Michael Otterson

Jorge Pardo
Jiyeon Park
Jennifer Pastor
Regent Pellerin
Raymond Pettibon
Richard Pettibone
Hirsch Perlman
Dan Peterman
Jerry Phillips
Ann Pibal
Adrian Piper
Johnny Pixchure
Cynthia Plaster Caster
Josh Podoll
Rebecca Potts
Richard Prince
Franklin Preston
Pruitt-Early
Charles Ray
Brent Reichman
Jamie Reid
Jason Reppert
Mark Resch
REX
Richard Rezac
Houston Ripley
Matthew Ritchie
David Robbins
Nathaniel Robinson
Michael Rodriguez
Marc Romano
Sheree Rose
Kay Rosen
Alexander Ross
Gerd Rothman
Ruth Rothschild
Allen Ruppersberg
Sherman Sam
Jimmy de Sana
Dan Sandin
Ellen Sandor
Rene Santos
Christopher Sasser
David Saunders
Nicolaus Schafhausen
Bill Seaman
David Sessions
Nancy Shaver
David Shaw
Jim Shaw
Ken Shaw
Rick Siggins
Martin Silverman
Raghubir Singh

Jennifer Sirey
Tom Skomski
Romain Slocombe
Oren Slor
Cary Smith
Joshua Smith
Ned Snider
Annie Sprinkle
Michael St. John
Haim Steinbach
Oona Stern
Hiroshi Sugimoto
A.K.Summers
Jan Sutcliffe
Taro Suzuki
Vincent Szarek
Michael K. Swenson
Mitchell Syrop
Alfredo Tadini
Gengoroh Tagame
Tony Tasset
Michael Tetherow
The Hun
Toadhouse
Motohiko Tokuta
Tom of Finland
Fred Tomaselli
John Torreano
Mark Travanti
Rosemarie Trockel
Lily van der Stokker
Tyler Vlahovich
Davor Vrankic
Jonathan Waterbury
Sally Webster
Robin Weglinski
James Welling
Lawrence Weiner
Alan Wiener
Hannah Wilke
Gavin Wilson
Kevin Wolff
Christopher Wool
Randy Wray
B. Wurtz
Rick X
Tamara Zahaykevich
Mel Ziegler

*I Only Want You to Love Me*
October 7-November 4, 1989
(*curated by Hilton Als, installation by Hilton Als and Darryl A.
Turner*) Camille Billops, James

Hamilton, Gina Harrell, Judy
Linn, Suzanne Miles, Adrian
Piper, Lorna Simpson, Darryl A.
Turner, James van der Zee

*The Moderns.* June 1-July 28,
1995 (*curated by Tony Payne*)
Judie Bamber, Bastille,
Matthew Benedict, Ross
Bleckner, Tom Bonauro,
Boneboyz, John Boskovitch, Jeff
Burton, Marcus Cafferty, Joe
Cavallaro, Sofia Coppola, Meg
Cranston, Louise Diedrich, Bart
Everly, Scott Ewalt, Seth Ferris,
Robert Flack, Pat Frantz, Eric
Freeman, General Idea, Nan
Goldin, Félix González-Torres,
Richard Hawkins, Jim Isermann,
Mike Kelley, Douglas Kolk,
Lauren Lesko, Scott Lifshutz,
Lovett/Codagnone, Robert
Mapplethorpe, Keith Mayerson,
Markus Morianz, Tony Payne,
Jack Pierson, Proctor/Renaldi,
REX, Aura Rosenberg, Tom of
Finland, Fernando Santangelo,
David Seidner, Hugh Steers,
Daniel Tull, James Vance, WAH,
Andy Warhol, Bruce Weber,
Chris Wilder.

*Candy Darling, Always a
Lady: Devotional Icons and
Memorabilia* May 17-June 21,
1997 (*organized by the Andy
Warhol Museum from the collection
of Jeremiah Newton, the Andy
Warhol Museum, and other lenders*)
anonymous, Robert Agriopoulos,
Sheyla Baykal, Peter Beard,
Cecil Beaton, Richard Bernstein,
Dagmar, Candy Darling, Walter
Diegold, Kenn Duncan, Robin
Drury, James Gossage, Bob
Gruen, George Haimsohn,
Philippe Halsman, Peter Hujar,
Jed Johnson, Ray Johnson,
Gerard Malanga, Billy Maynard,
Jack Mitchell, Laura Rubin,
Francesco Scavullo, Irene Vilhar,
Andy Warhol

*The three preceding exhibitions
were the only shows at Feature
not organized by Hudson.*

*Power to the People*
May 1, 2010

Joshua Abelow
Tish Abelow
Bill Adams
John Adastra
Steven Alexander
Candida Alvarez
Renata de Andrade
Lorenzo De Los Angeles
Anonymous
Anonymous
Rosaire Appel
Amy Bassin
Gary Batty
Paul Baumann
Lisa Beck
Nancy Becker
Lindsay Benedict
Mel Bernstine
Chris Bertholf
Jeffrey Bishop
Dike Blair
Martin Bland
Richard Brachman
Paul Brainard
Jesse Bransford
Mai Braun
Sarah Brenneman
Bruce Brosnan
Dinton Zilworth and
 Gary Brotmeyer
Alex Brown
Hoyt Brown
Pam Butler
Janusz Welin and
 James Campbell
Janet Carkeek
Kris Chatterson
Gina de la Chesnaye
Edmund Chia
Amanda Church
Laura Cincotta
Holly Coulis
Scott Cousins
Emma Coyle
Mark Cranford
Fred Cray
Carl D'Alvia
Taylor Davis
Jason Denholm
Eric Dever

Susan Dory
Jim Duesing
Ula Einstein
Cara Enteles
Jay Erker
Jake Ewert
Bruno Fazzolari
Tony Feher
Amy Feldman
Jeri Felix
Carl Ferrero
Julia Fish
Robert Flynt
Robert Fontanelli
Jean Foos
Alyssa L. Foos
Pamela Fraser
David Frye
Ted Gahl
Jan Galligan
J.J. Garfinkel
J.C. Garrett
Robin Gaynes-Bachman
Allison Gildersleeve
Glenn Goldberg
Bobby Goldman
Tamara Gonzales
Janine Gordon
Sam Gordon
Gray
Jonah Groeneboer
Carl Gunhouse
Léonie Guyer
Charles Hagen
Irene Hanenbergh
Jan Harrison
Joshua Hart
Jonathan Hartshorn
Halsey Hathaway
Kylie Heidenheimer
Thomas Hellstrom
Molly Herman
Molly Heron
Daniel Hesidence
Peter Hildebrand
Heather Holden
Doug Holst
Mamie Holst
George Horner
Ridley Howard
James Huang
Peter Huttinger
John Jackson

Franck André Jamme
Bill Jenkins
Daniel Jennings
Ivelisse Jiménez
Michael St. John
Howard Johnson
Jerome Johnson
Clint Jukkala
Diane June
Troy June
Vivian Kahra
Dennis Kardon
Erika Keck
Patrick Keesey
Richard Kern
Charles Kessler
Julia Klein
Bernard Klevickas
Elisabeth Kley
Karla Knight
Nicholas Knight
Todd Knopke
Rosalie Knox
Anne Koch
Bill Komoski
Kinke Kooi
Scooter LaForge
Charles Lahti
Nick Lamia
Kevin Larmon
Heidi Lau
Diana Lawrence
Michael Lazarus
Gwyneth Leech
John Fekner and Don Leicht
Elisa Lendvay
Jon Leon
Ellen Levy
Judy Linn
Patrice Lorenz
Eliza Loring
Giles Lyon
Doug Henders and
   Staci MacKenzie
Gina Magid
Vicki Mansoor
Adam Marnie
Lael Marshall
Steve McCall
Daniel McDonald
Roy McMakin
Douglas Melini
Tracy Miller

Billy Miller
John Mills
Gregory Montreuil
Gene Moreno
Andrea Morganstern
Sean Moyer
Lillian Mulero
Naoto Nakagawa
Nancy
Zach Needler
Joan Nelson
Joe Heaps Nelson
Katherine Newbegin
Laura Newman
Jessica Nissen
Josh C. Nusbaum
C.J. Nye
Kylin O'Brien
Bobbie Oliver
Jeff Ono
John Ortiz
Ted O'Sullivan
Michael Ottersen
Jiyeon Park
Stefano W. Pasquini
Gary Petersen
Jerry Phillips
Sarah Nicole Phillips
Ann Pibal
Jordan Pike
Esther Podemski
Nigel Poor
Rebecca Potts
Don Powley
Jeanne Quinn
Kazimira Rachfal
Kanishka Raja
Juli Raja
Max Razdow
Beth Reitmeyer
Janet Rente
Richard Rezac
Nathaniel Robinson
Michael Rodriguez
Kay Rosen
Lynn Rosenfeld
Dirk Rowntree
David Rubin
Donna Ruff
Jackie Saccoccio
Jesse Sadia
Amy Sarkisian
Julie Sass

Patricia Satterlee
Eric Schnell
Claudia Schwalb
Stuart Servetar
Beth Servetar
Nancy Shaver
David Shaw
Andrea Shear
Charles Shedden
James Sheehan
Christy Singleton
Jennifer Sirey
Patricia Smith
Emily Smith
Cary Smith
Ben Snead
MiYoung Sohn
Murphy Spicer
Ryan Steadman
Gary Stephan
Oona Stern
Steel Stillman
Suzanne Stroebe
Barbara Sullivan
Glenn Suokko
Taro Suzuki
Theresa Swanick
Earl Swanigan
Mike Swenson
Adrian Ting
John Torreano
Weston Ulfig
Liz-N-Val
Nichole van Beek
Tyler Vlahovich
Michael Voss
Ryan M. Walker
William Walker
Keith Walsh
Jan Wandrag
Oliver Warden
Sally Webster
Bill Weiss
Jerry van ve Wiele
Alan Wiener
Gavin Wilson
Margaret Withers
Beatrice Wolert
B. Wurtz
Mie Yim
Tamara Zahaykevich
Jeff Zimmerman
Brenda Zlamany

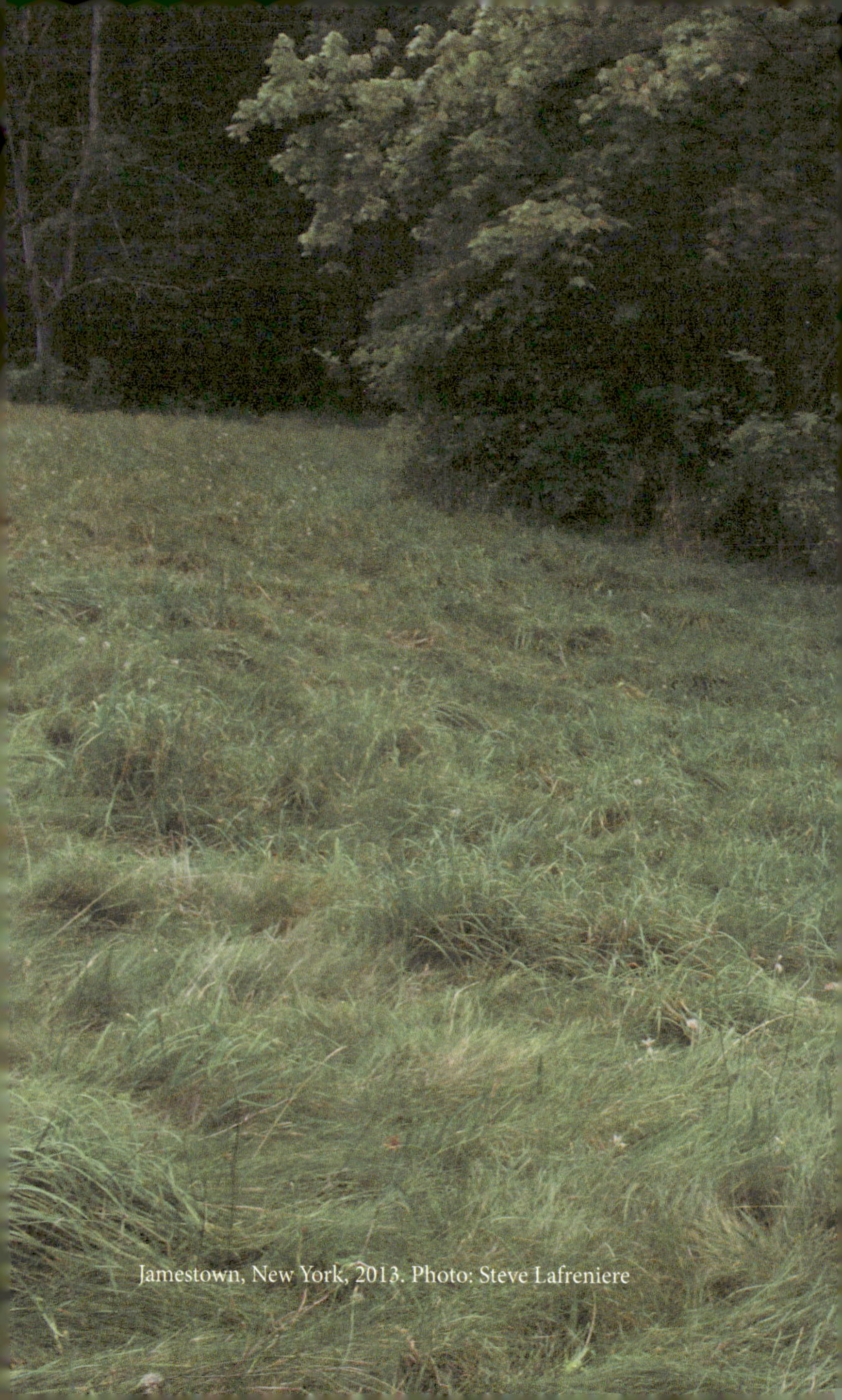
Jamestown, New York, 2013. Photo: Steve Lafreniere

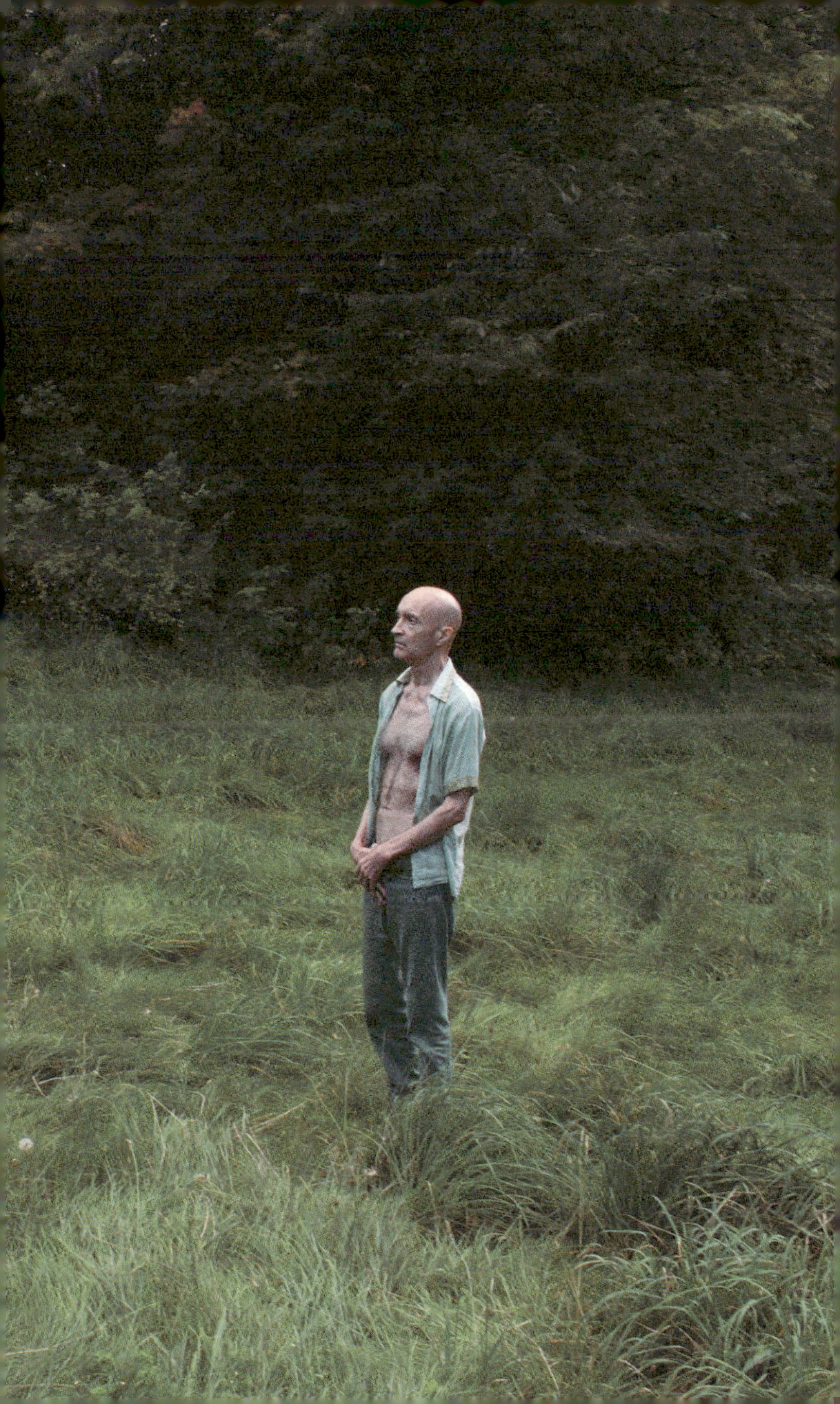

## ACKNOWLEDGMENTS

I must express my deep gratitude to all who spoke and wrote so intimately about our departed friend. It confirmed to me that Hudson's memory burns bright among us all. Particular thanks to his sister Patricia for supplying details and stories of his childhood and younger years.

Further thank yous go to James White for contributing the piercing cover portrait of Hudson; to Jerry Phillips for the drawing of Hudson's ubiquitous written salutation, "Hello"; to James Pedersen and David Shaw for cheerfully answering an endless stream of detailed queries; to Dike Blair for permitting us to include his revealing interview with Hudson; to Michael St. John for the superb portrait; to Charles Ray for the wonderful, concise drawing; to Judy Linn for the handsome photograph of Hudson adjusting his collar; to John Richard Allen for the photo of Hudson with G.B. Jones; to Arthur Fournier for the scans of *Farm* issues; to Kelly King for our email exchanges; to Joel Westendorf for the technical expertise; to Jordan Stein for the writerly advice; and to Dan Fox for the sharp-eyed copyediting skills.

Finally, enormous kudos to Julia Klein, Soberscove Press publisher/editor/majordomo, for her months of patient labor helping me shape this project. I could not have found a more sympathetic home for a book about Hudson and Feature than Soberscove.